EGGBERT
WHAT'LL I BE
WHEN I
GROW UP?

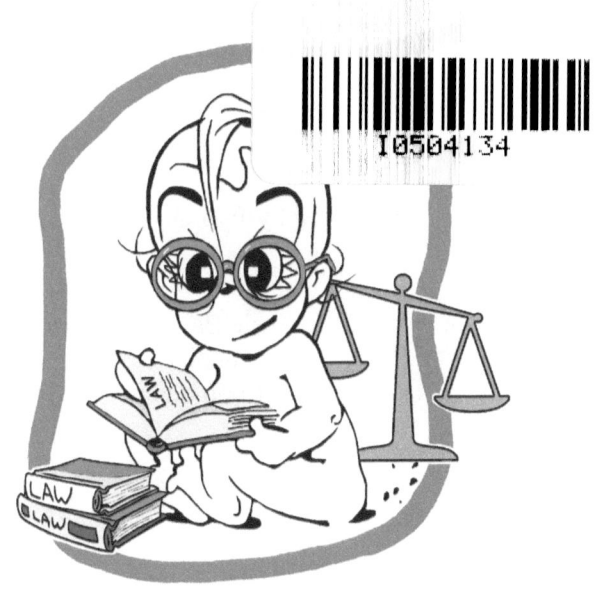

Based on
Cartoons by LAF

EGGBERT
WHAT'LL I BE
WHEN I
GROW UP?

A brand new edition with new cartoons
Based on the original cartoons

Printed with permission

Re-Created by Judi Quelland

With gratitude to Susie Barker Lavenson,
Daughter of Percy Barker, publisher of the original
Eggbert cartoon books

THEY'RE BACK . . .
AND WITH 92 <u>NEW</u> CARTOONS!

Join **Eggbert** and his sister **Eggberta** as they ponder over what's going to be in their future in this book of brand new cartoons. They are based on the delightful Eggbert cartoons from so many years ago. However, it's not all serious with these two charismatic characters ... there's plenty of playtime too!

All these new cartoons were created as a labor of love for a pair of impish offspring who have delighted so many moms- and dads-to-be for a couple generations.

This book is a representation of the original Eggbert and Eggberta cartoons and it will keep the expectant Mom & Dad laughing all the way from the beginning of Mom's pregnancy right to the big day when their little one enters the world, and beyond ...

As always, wishing all Moms and Dads love, joy & fulfillment, and we provide this collection of cartoons as forever proof that humor is the best medicine in the world. Enjoy!

You will also enjoy these other
Eggbert books:

Eggbert

Eggbert and Eggberta

Inside Eggbert

Eggbert's Diary for a Lady-in-Waiting

Eggbert's Advice to the Love-Born

Eggbert's Countdown for the Expectant

Father

Strictly Fresh Eggbert

Eggbert Belly Laughs

Eggbert Easy Over

All of the above are faithful re-publications of the
Original Eggbert books

EGGBERT

WHAT'LL I BE
WHEN I
GROW UP?

ADULT HUMOR
FOR MOMS-TO-BE

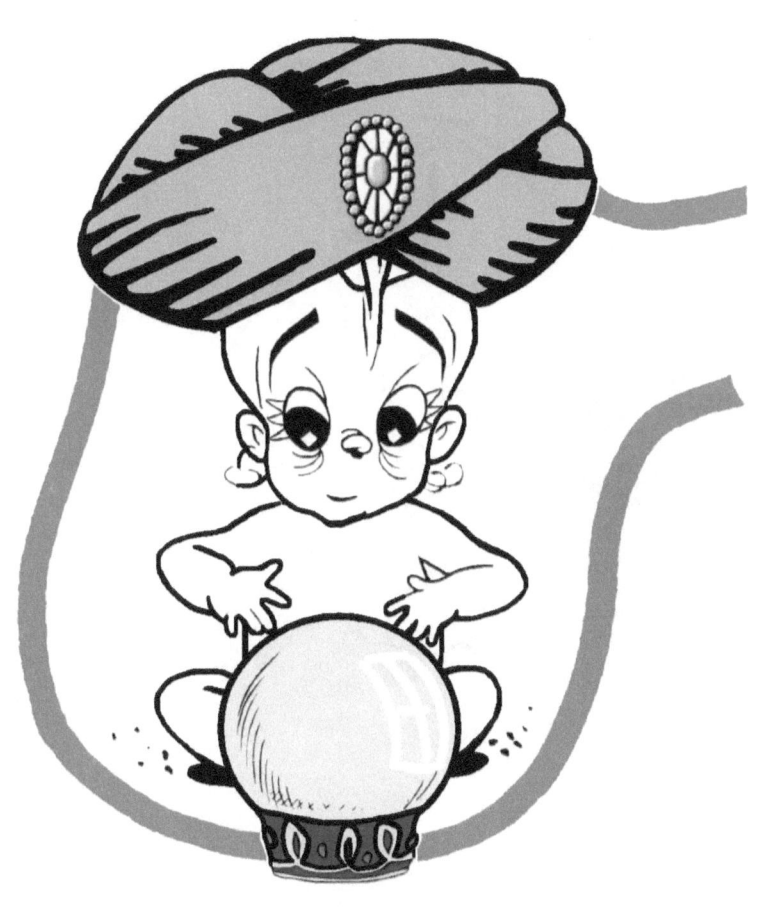

WHAT'LL I BE
WHEN I GROW UP ?

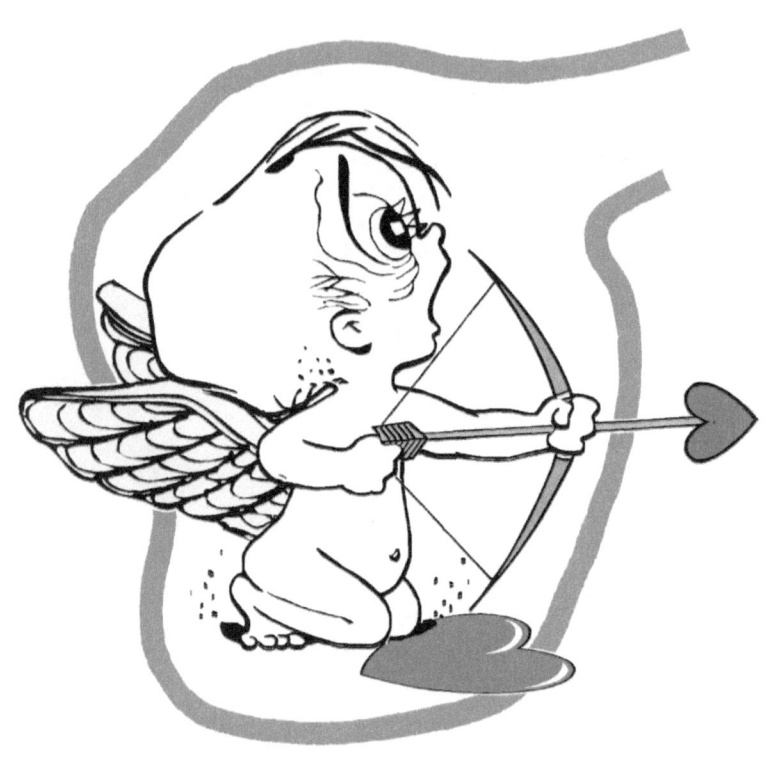

MA, YOU MEAN SINCE I'M
ALREADY HERE, POP DOESN'T
NEED CUPID'S ARROW?
OKAY.

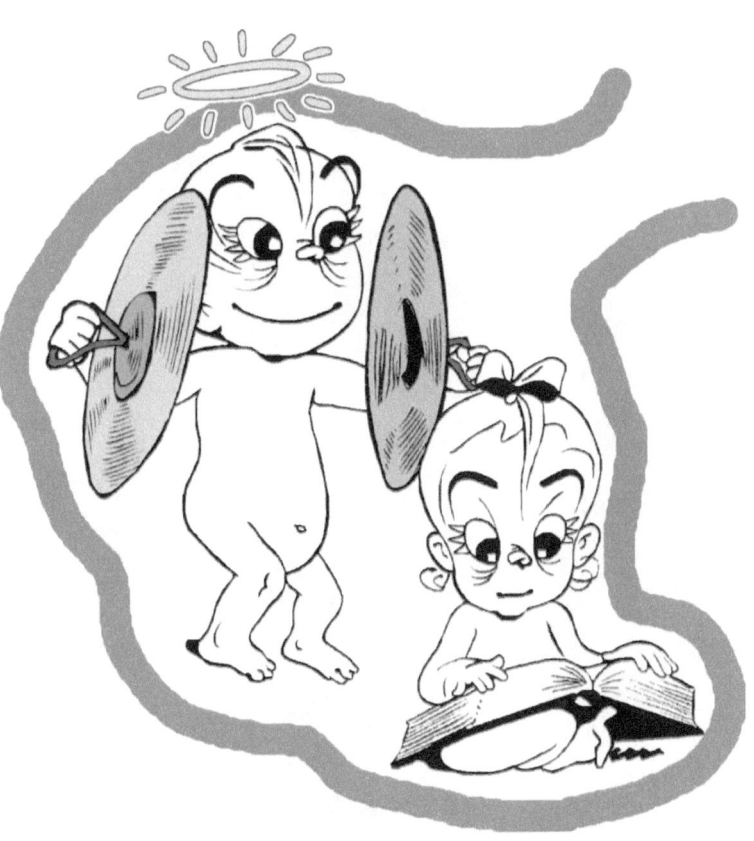

IF I DO THIS, I'M GONNA BE IN
SO-O-O-O MUCH TROUBLE! (HEH,HEH!)

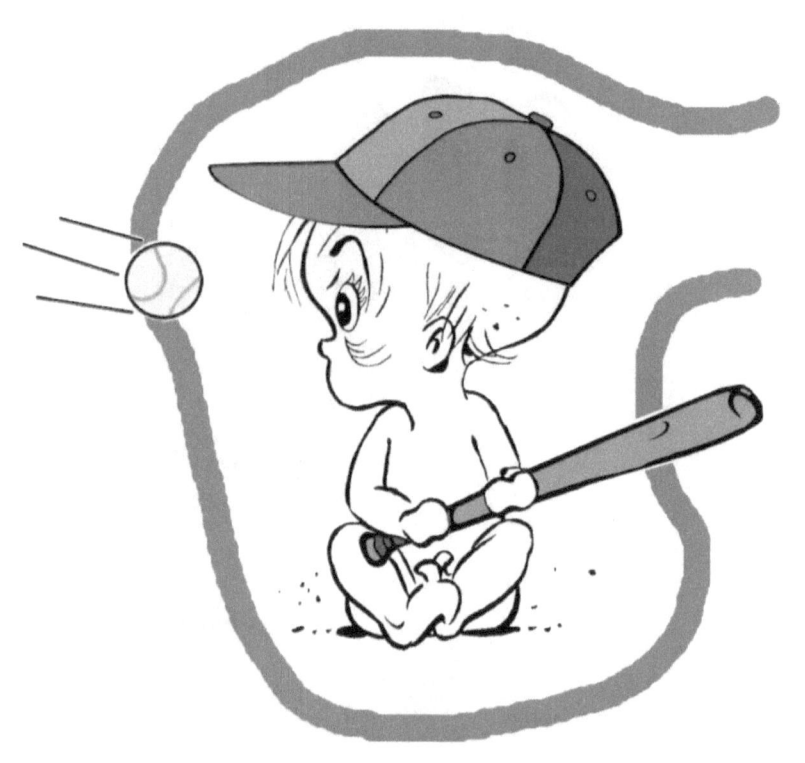

IN BASEBALL, YOU REALLY
GOTTA KEEP YOUR EYE
ON THE BALL !

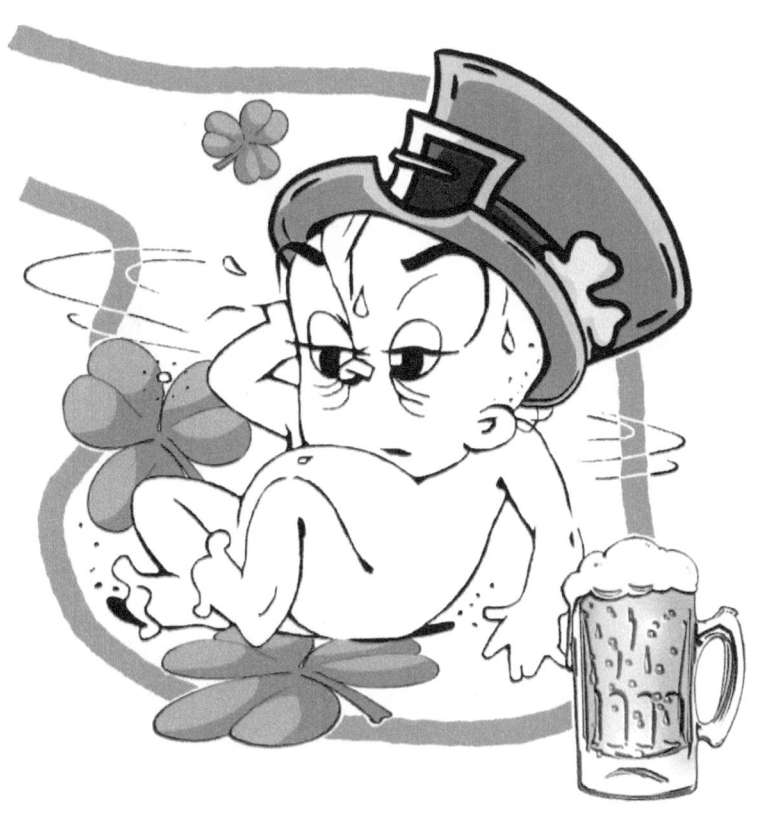

HEY, MA ... LAY OFF
THE GREEN BEER !

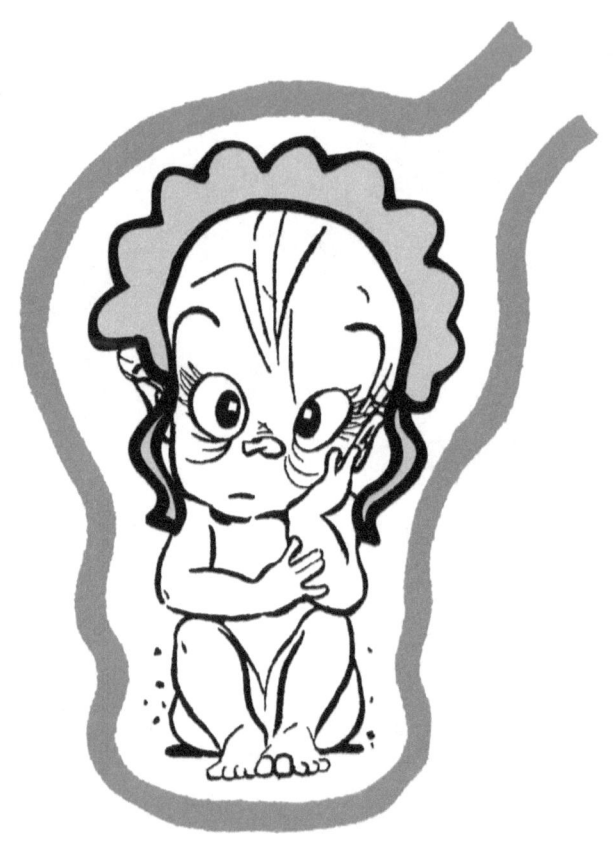

DO I HAFTA WEAR THIS ?
(I RECKON IT'S BETTER THAN A HEADBAND!)

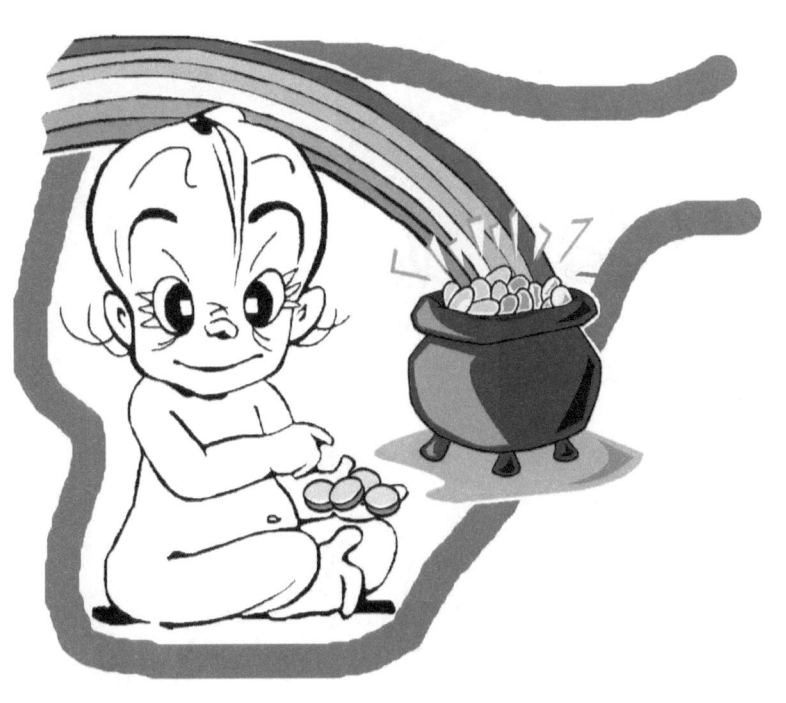

POT 'O GOLD, HUH ?
MA SAYS AFTER ALL THE
GREEN BEER, POP NEEDS A
DIFFERENT KIND OF POT !

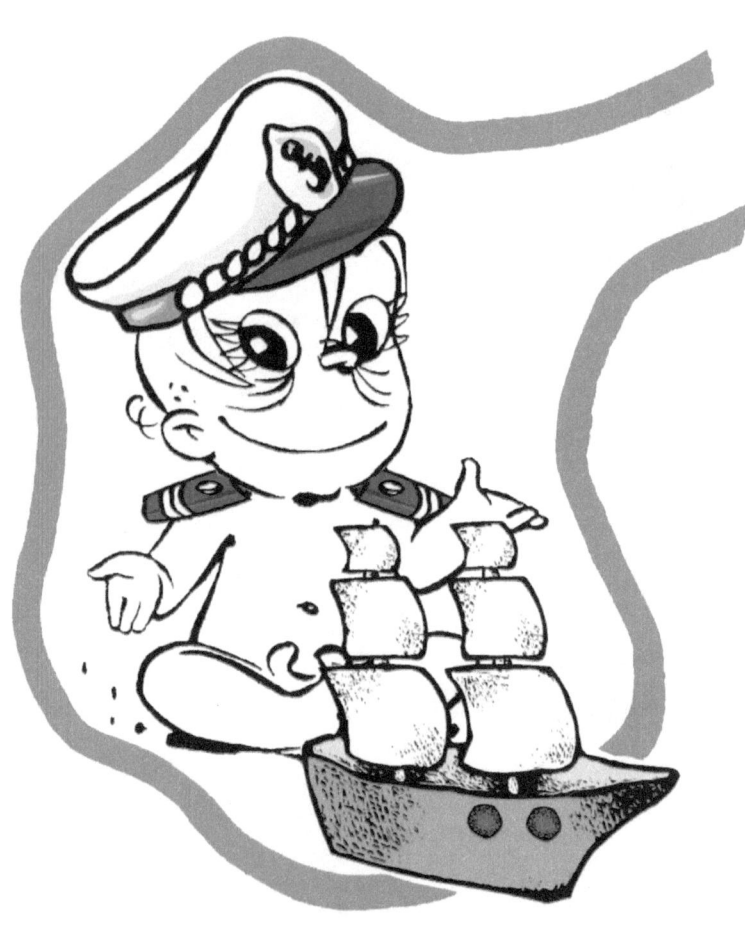

JOIN THE NAVY ...
SEE THE WORLD ...
REALLY ?

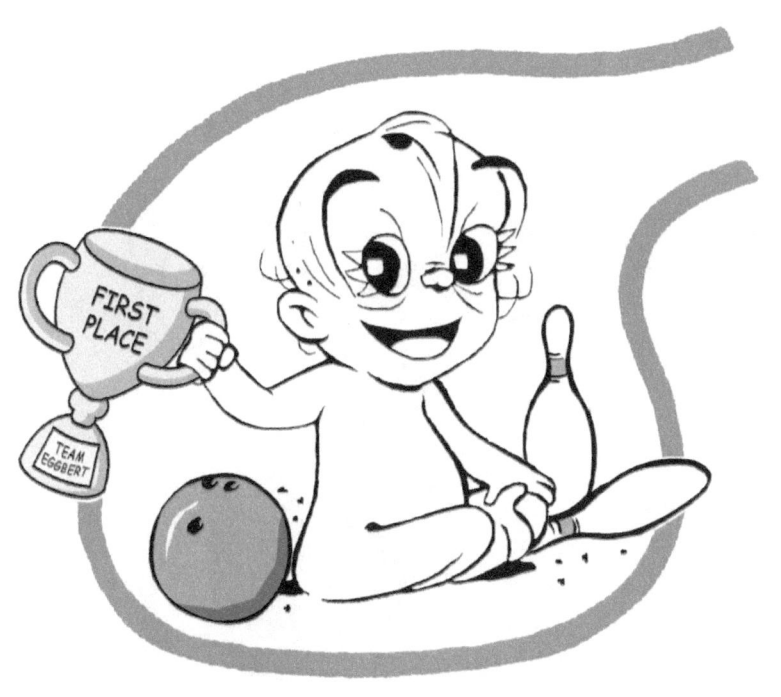

POP SAYS HE GOES BOWLING
FOR THE BEER.
I LIKE THE TROPHIES !

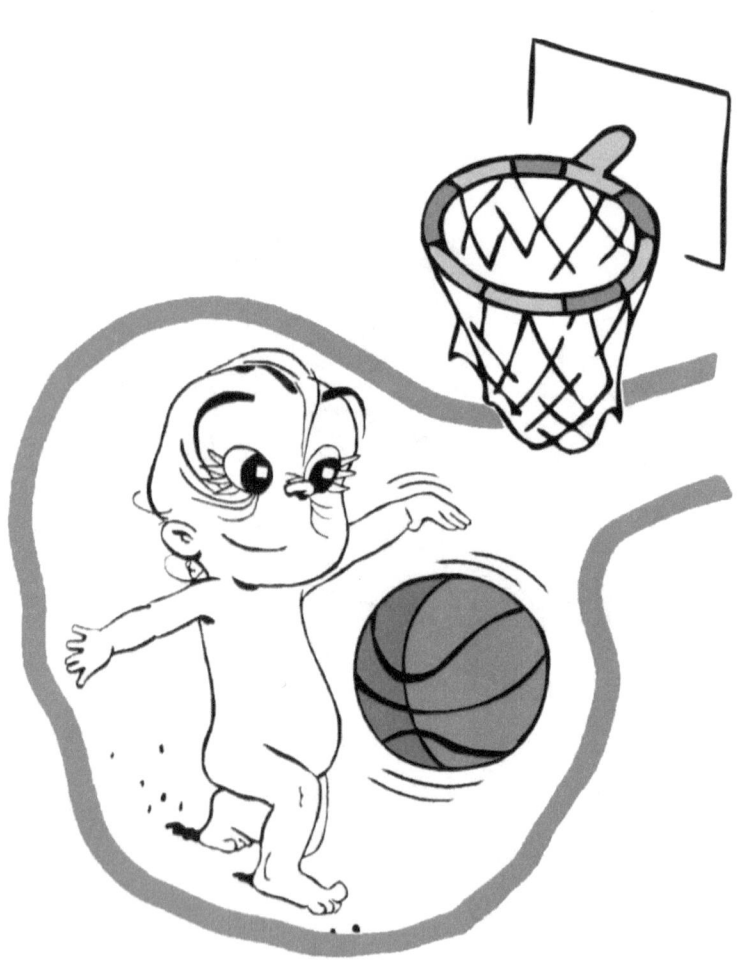

I'LL BE GREAT AT THIS ...
I CAN ALREADY DRIBBLE !

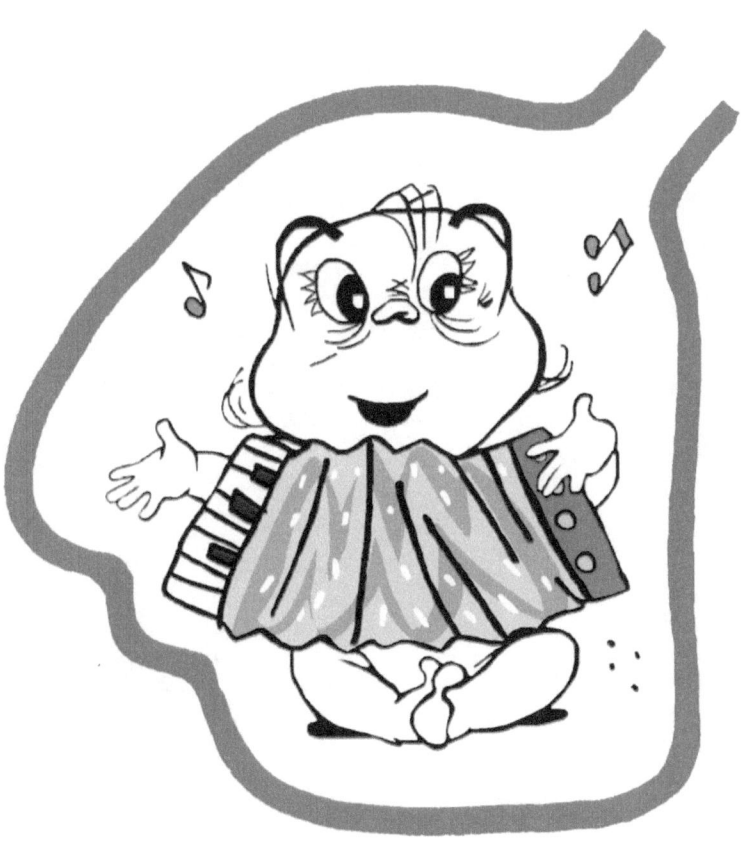

..AND A 1, AND A 2 . . .
HEY ... ANYBODY REMEMBER
LAWRENCE WELK ?

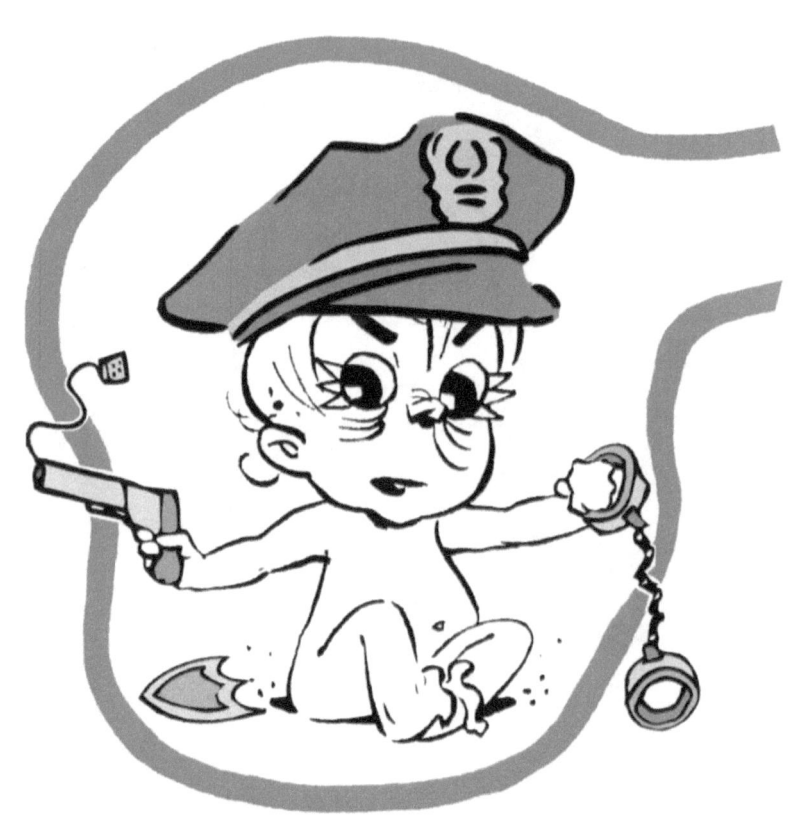

I'LL JUST HAVE TO ARREST YOU
FOR NOT BRINGING MY DONUTS!

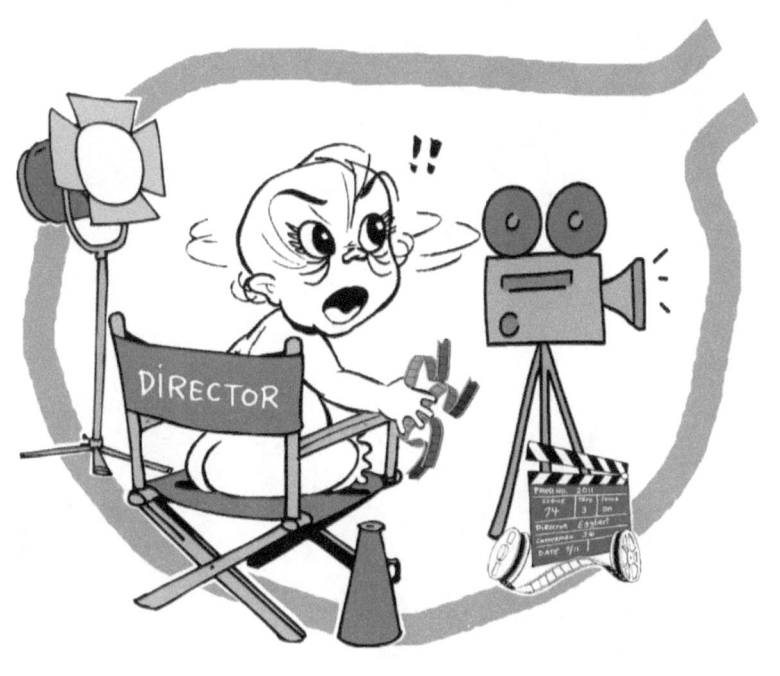

HEY ... I'M THE ONE WHO GETS TO
YELL "ACTION!"

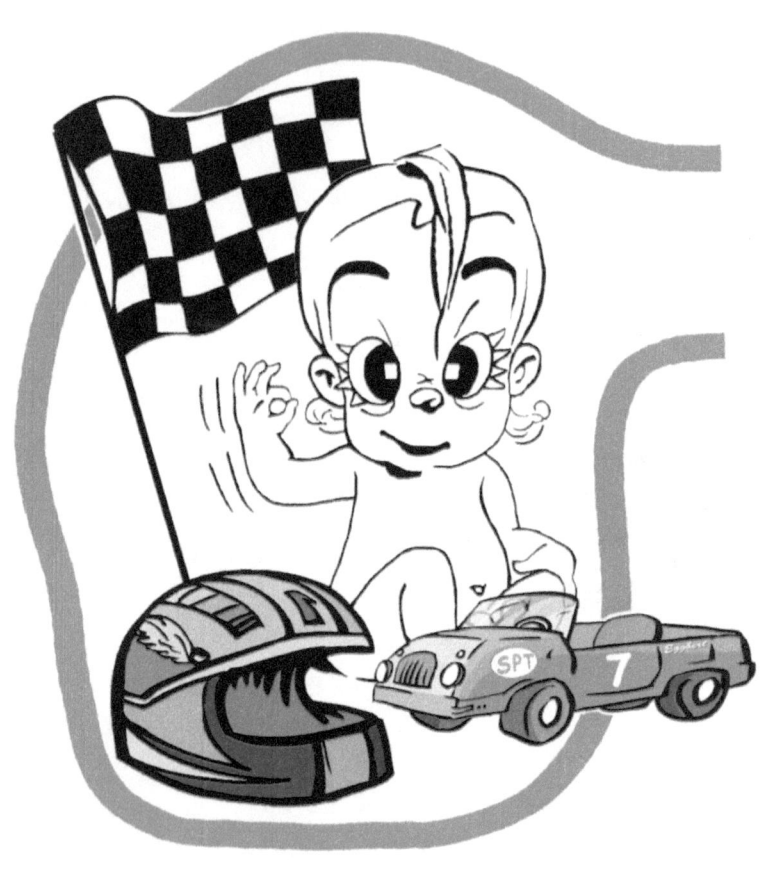

I'M A CINCH TO DRIVE
FOR NASCAR !

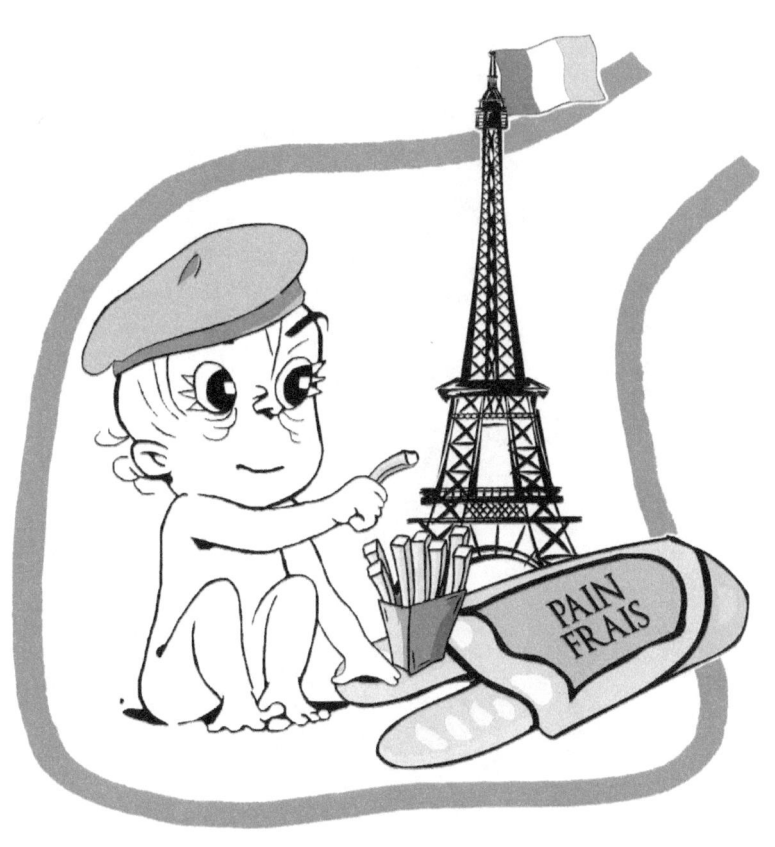

JE SUIS EGGBERT ET J'AIME TOUT FRANÇAIS

(I AM EGGBERT AND I LIKE EVERYTHING FRENCH)

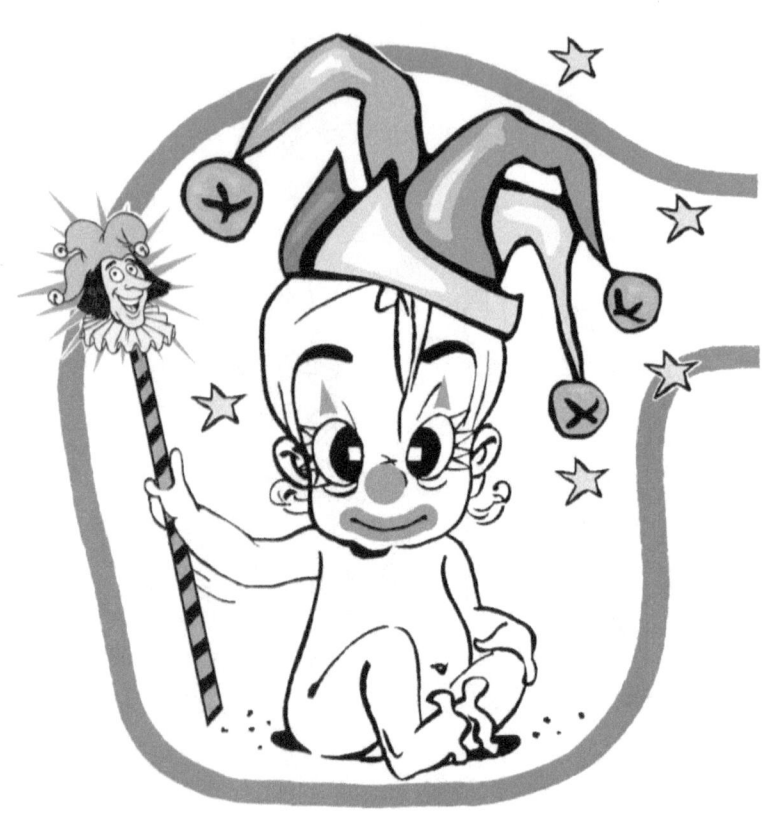

**MAYBE I'LL
JOIN A CIRCUS!**

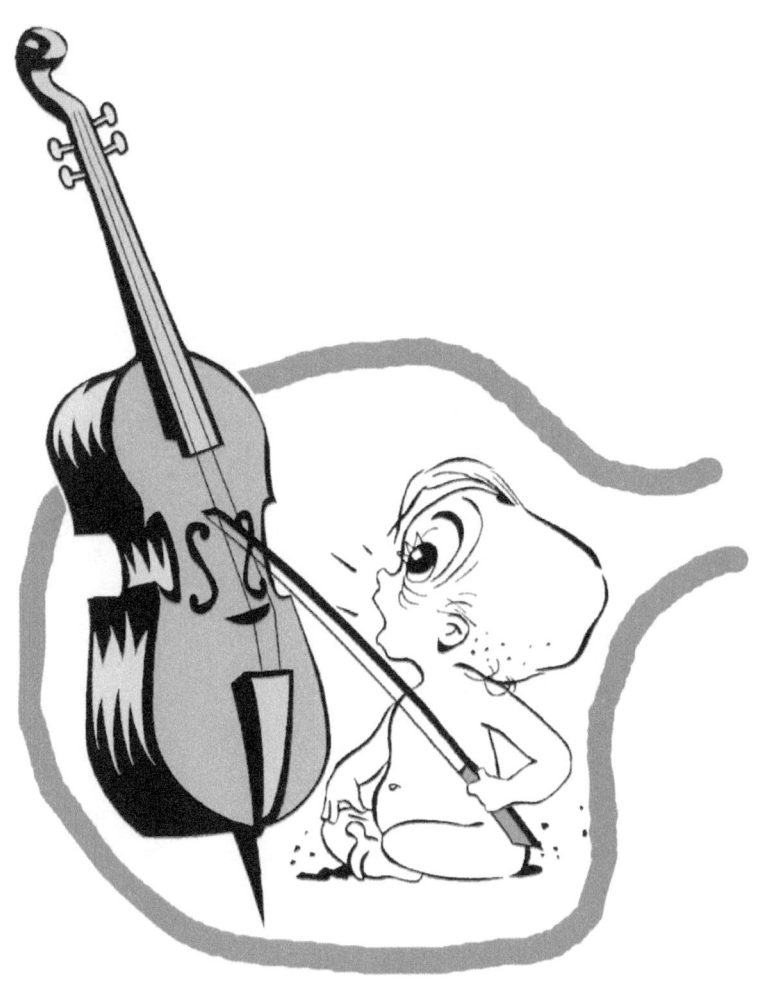

THIS THING LOOKS LIKE
A VIOLIN ON STEROIDS !

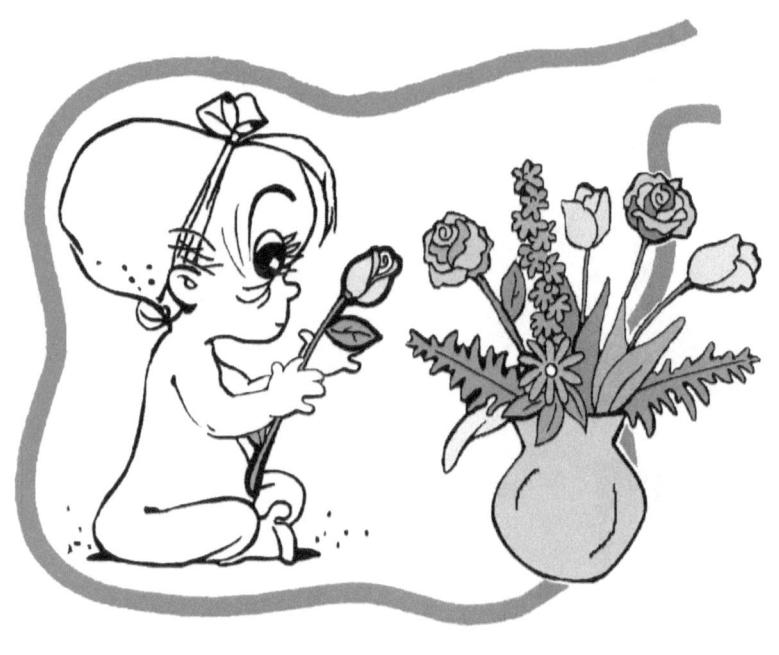

I HOPE MOM LIKES THE FLOWERS
I GOT HER FOR MY BIRTHDAY!

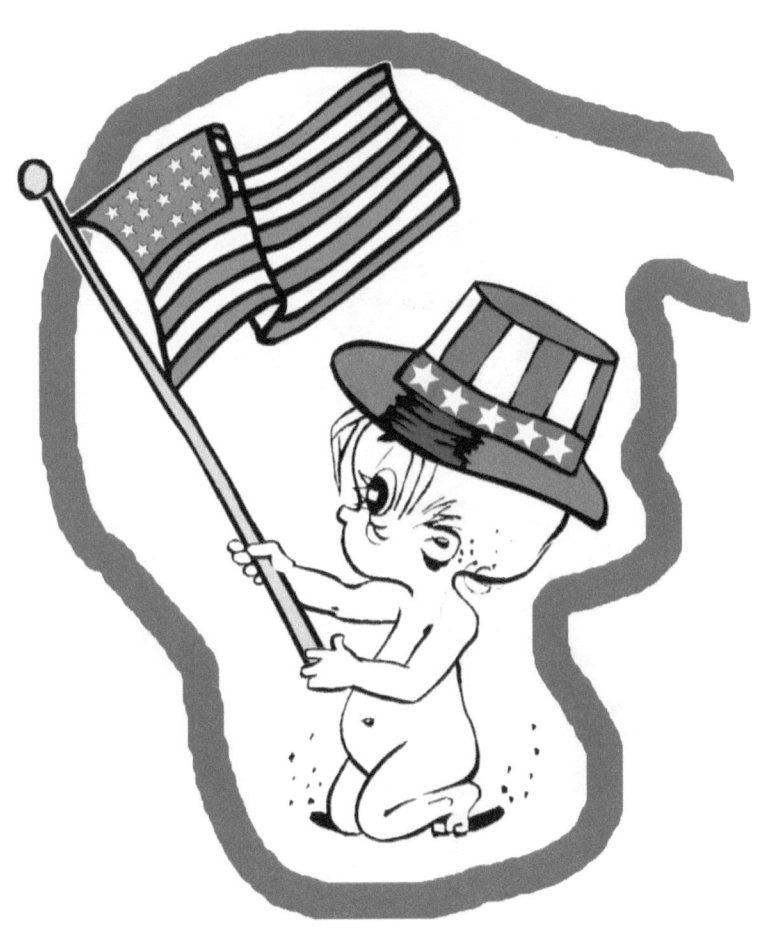

MOM & POP ALREADY TAUGHT ME
TO <u>ALWAYS</u> SUPPORT
THE TROOPS!

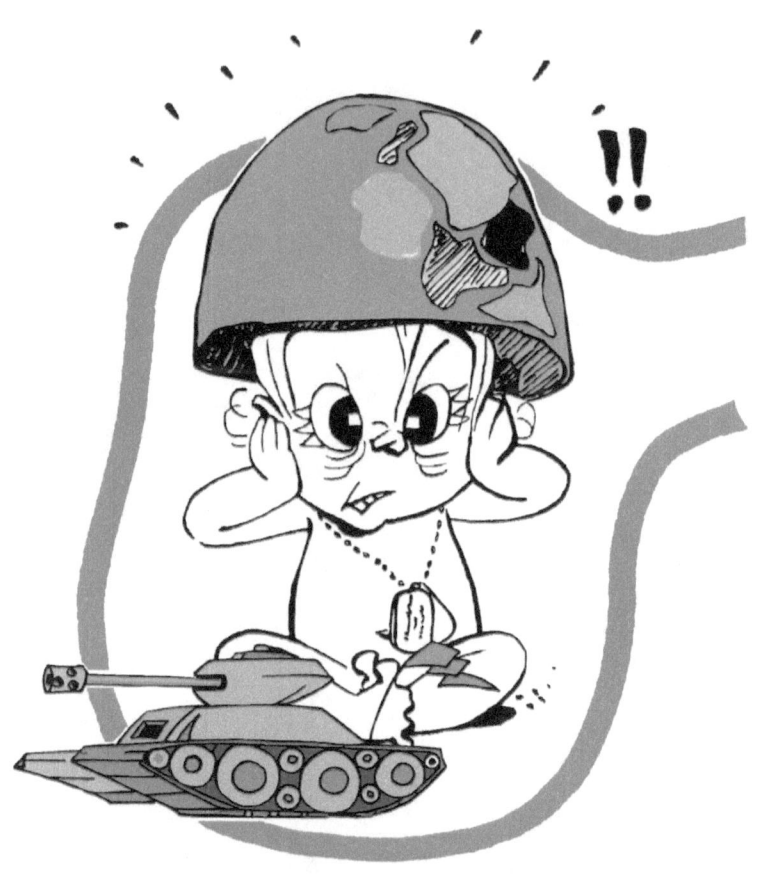

GEEZ, MOM ! I KNEW YOU WORE
COMBAT BOOTS, BUT I NEVER
THOUGHT THIS PLACE WOULD BE
SO <u>NOISY</u> !

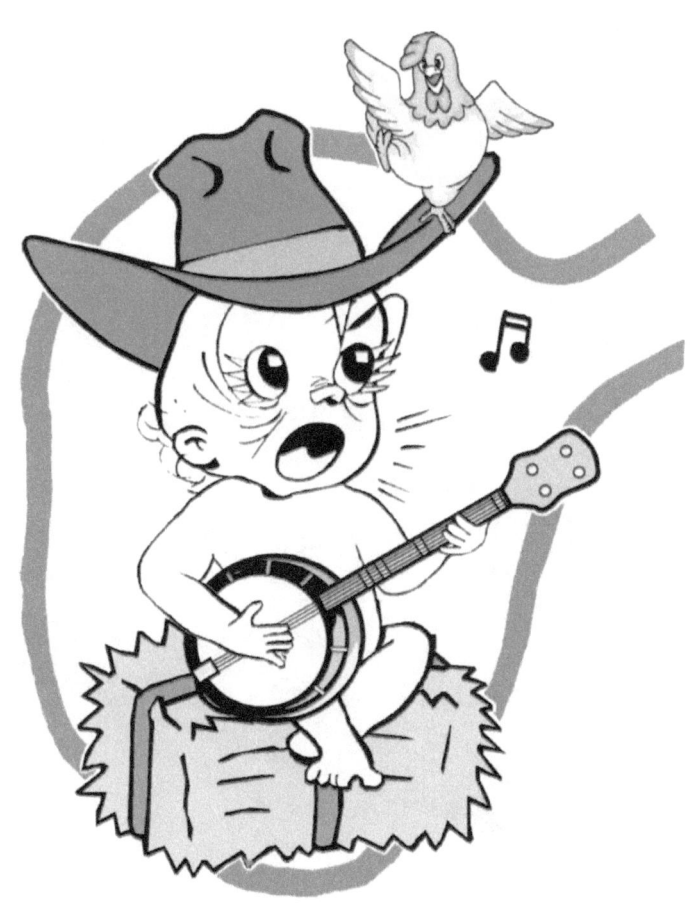

MOVE OVER, GARTH ...
I'M HEADED FOR THE
GRAND OL' OPRY !

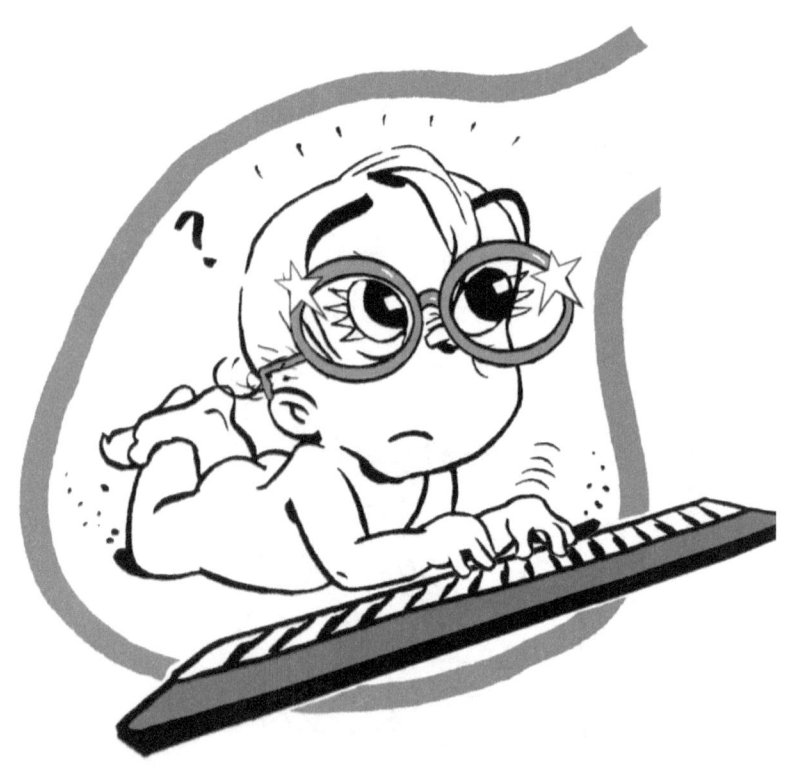

I WONDER IF THIS IS HOW
ELTON JOHN GOT STARTED.

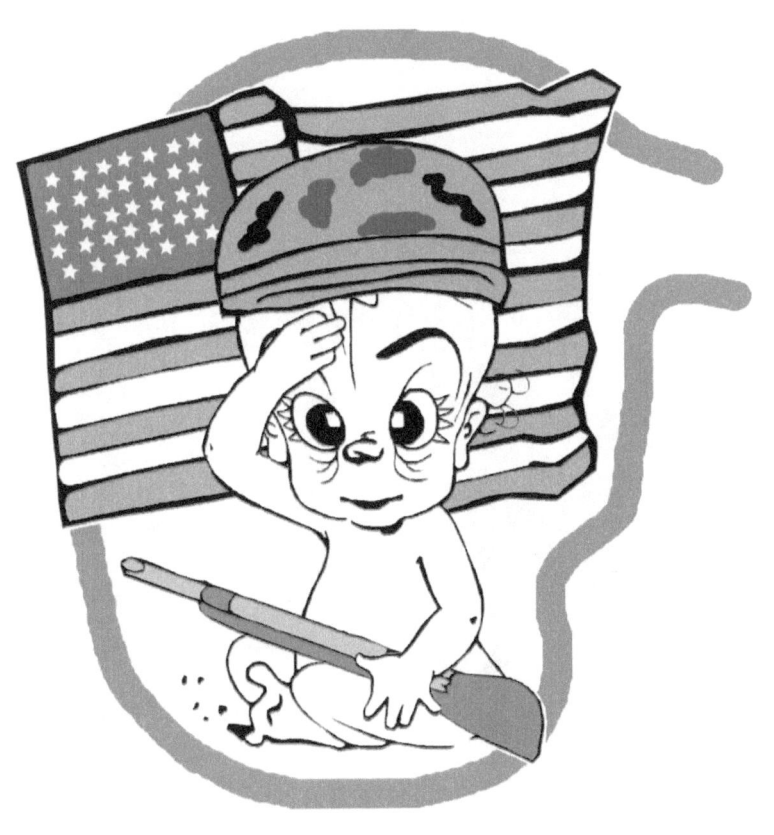

PRACTICING MY
SALUTE TO THE TROOPS !

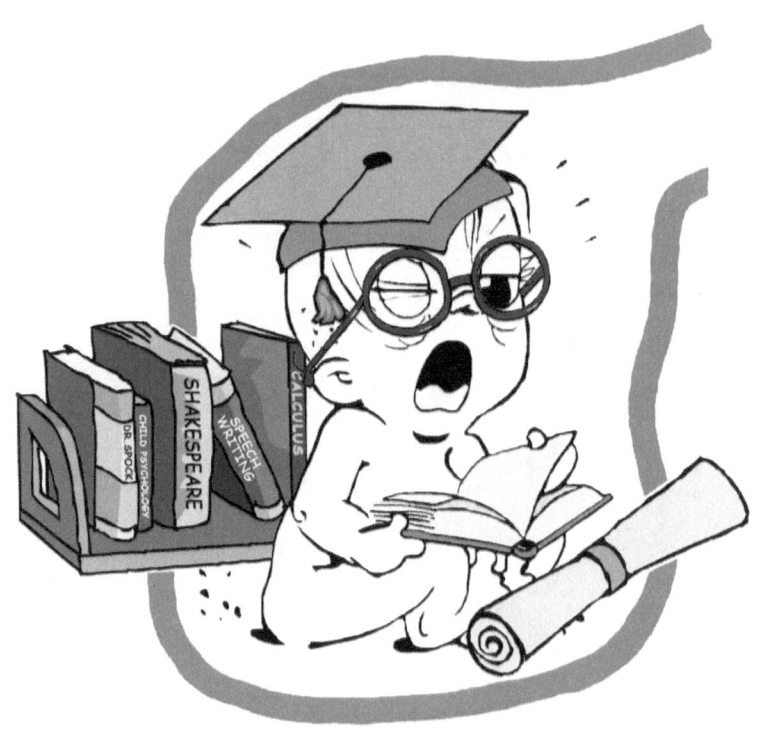

I'M GLAD MA FINALLY GRADUATED...
NO MORE ALL-NIGHTERS FOR US !

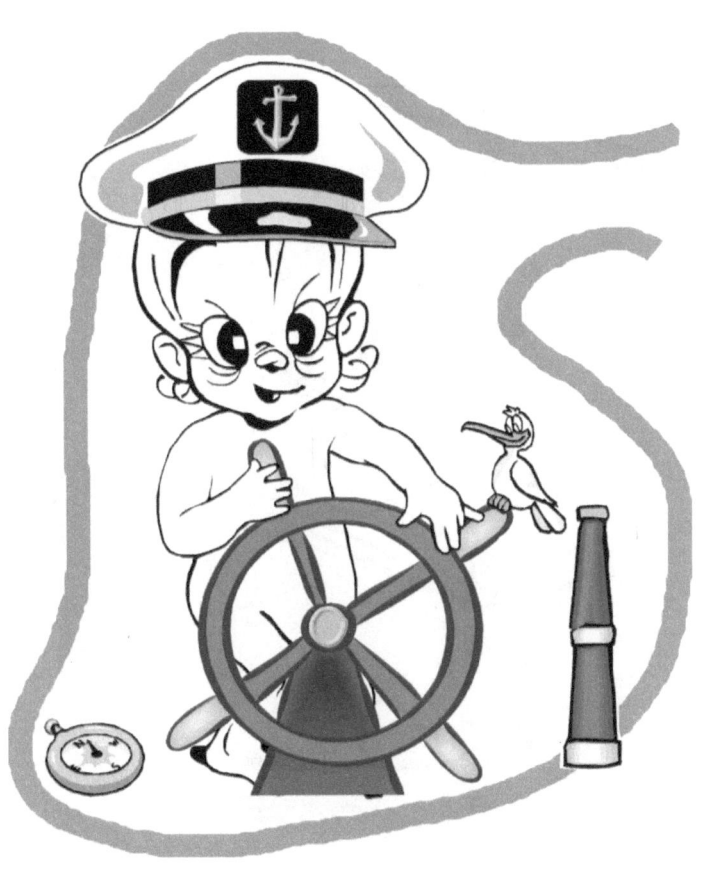

IS THIS HOW BLACKBEARD
GOT HIS START?

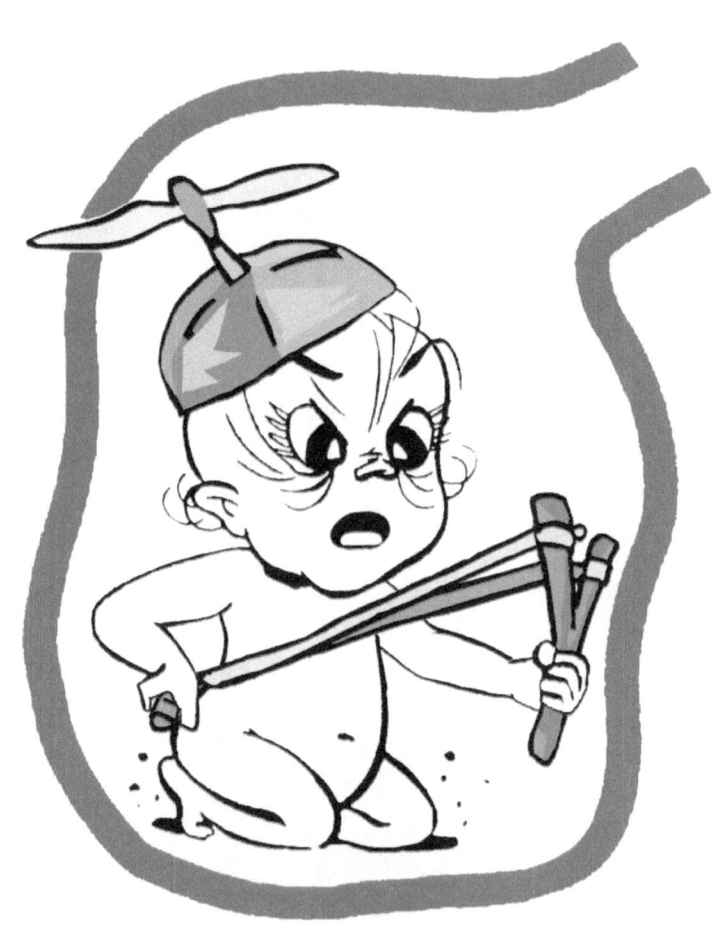

HEY POP ... WHEN MA SAYS "NO"
SHE MEANS "NO" !

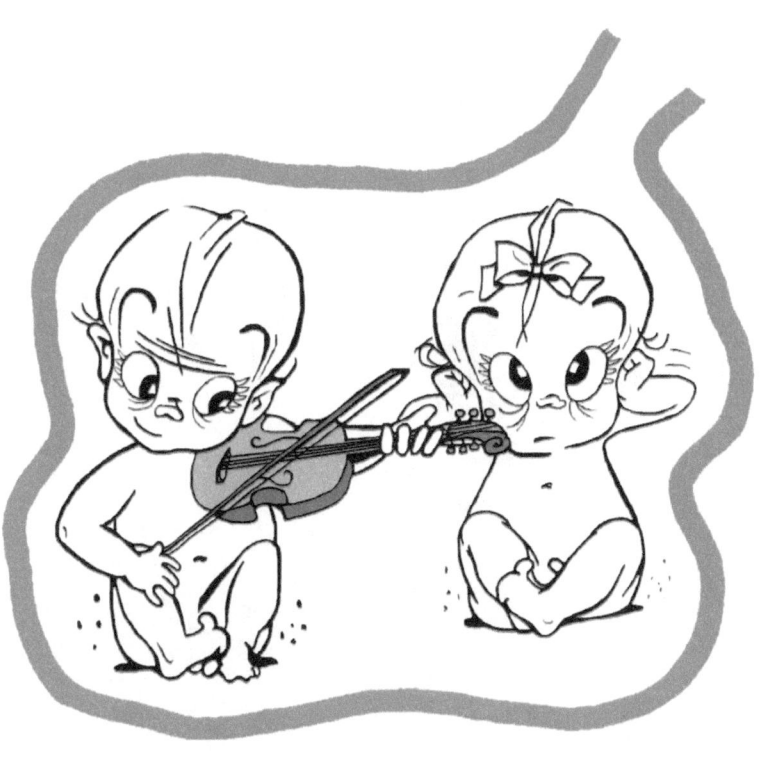

SORRY SIS, VIOLINS SCREECH A LOT BEFORE
YOU CAN FIND THE SWEET MUSIC

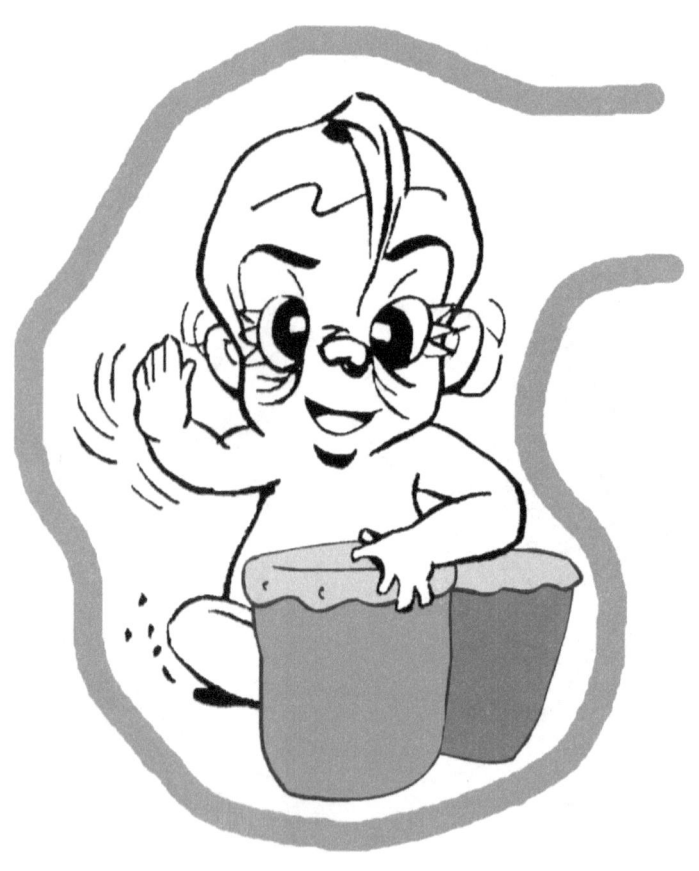

BONGOS ARE SURE A LOT EASIER TO
CARRY AROUND THAN A BASS DRUM!

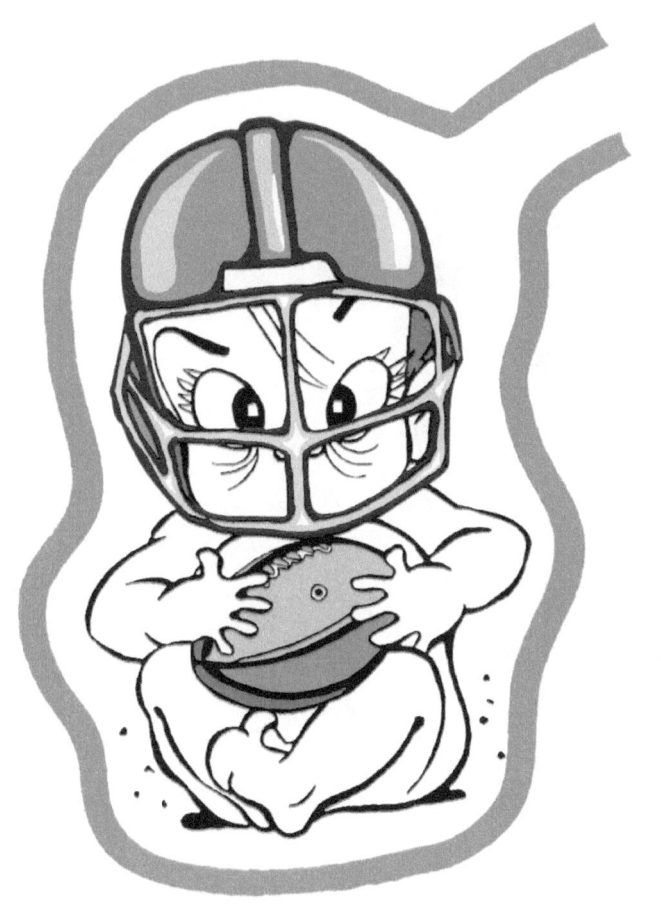

SCOUTS, DRAFTS, FREE AGENCY,
CONTRACTS, MEDIA EVENTS ...
WHEN DO WE GET TO PLAY FOOTBALL?

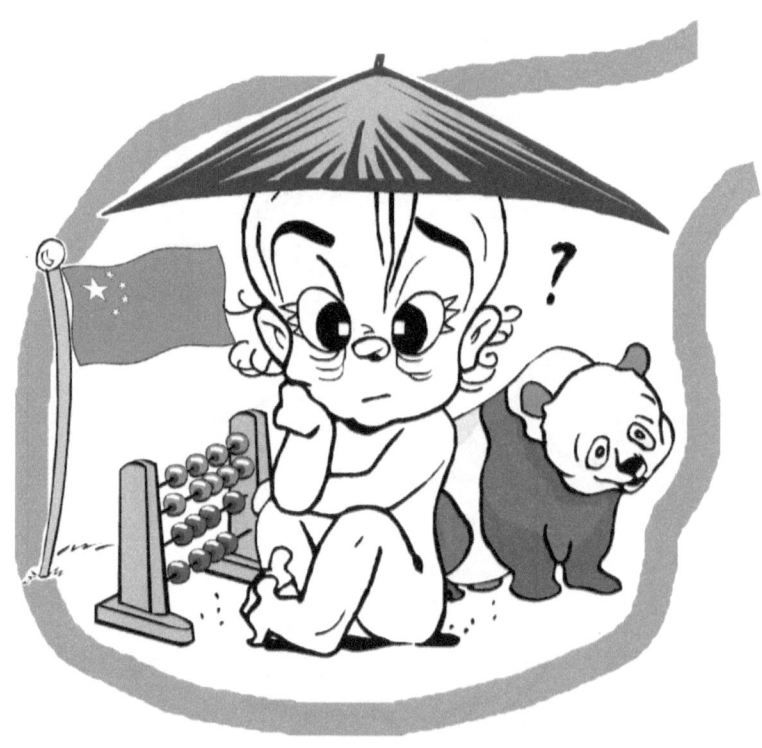

FOR THE LIFE OF ME, I CAN'T
FIGURE OUT THIS ABACUS !

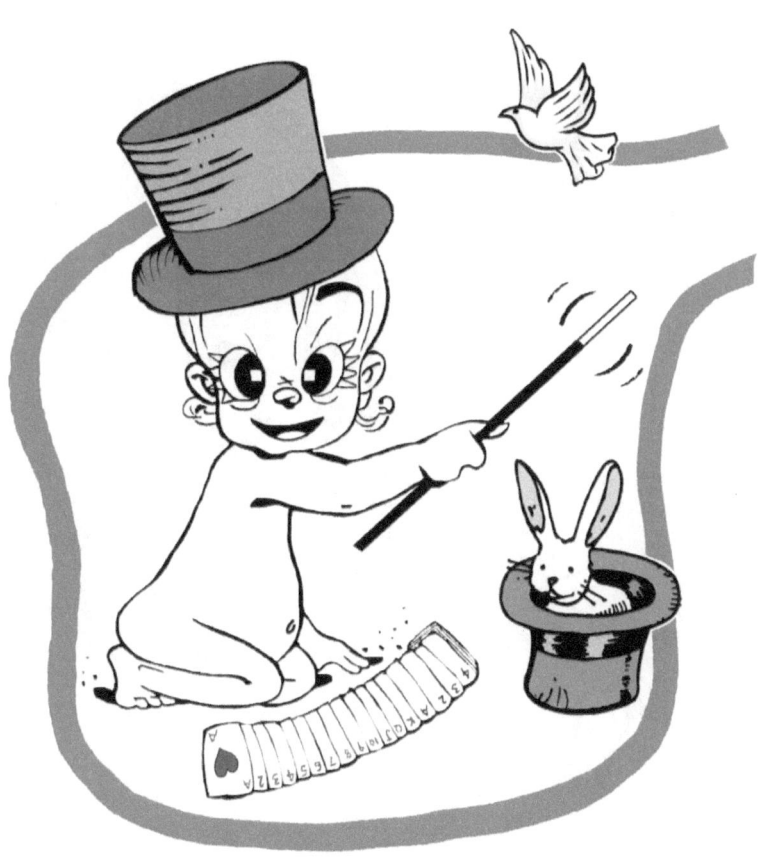

GOTTA PRACTICE FOR THE
BIG TALENT CONTEST!

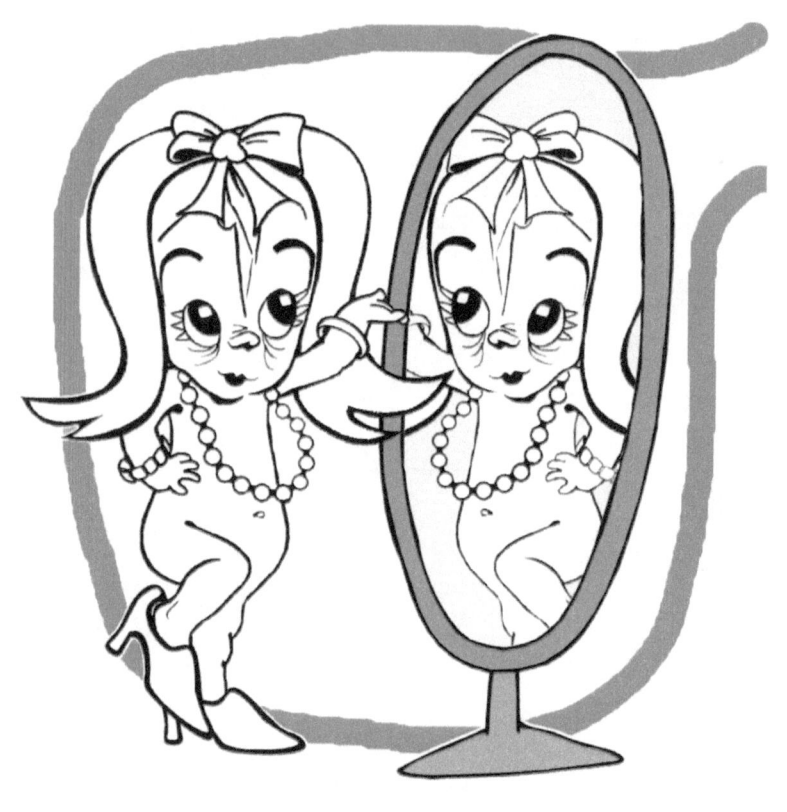

I JUST MIGHT BE THE
NEXT TOP MODEL !

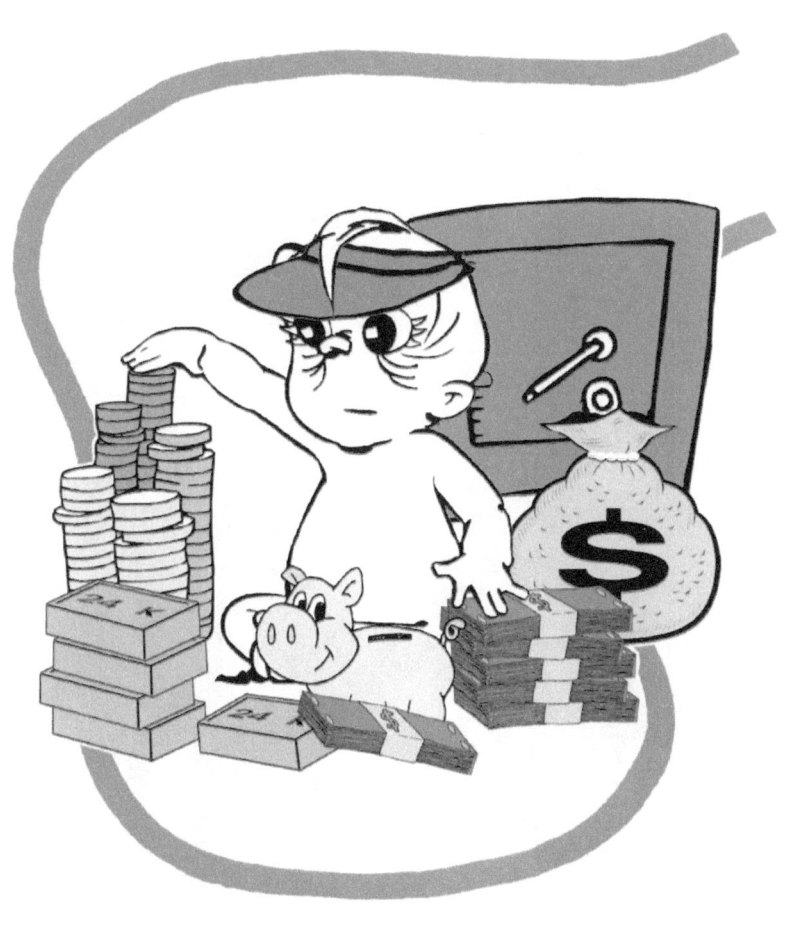

I THINK I NEED AN ADDING
MACHINE AND THEN A COMPUTER

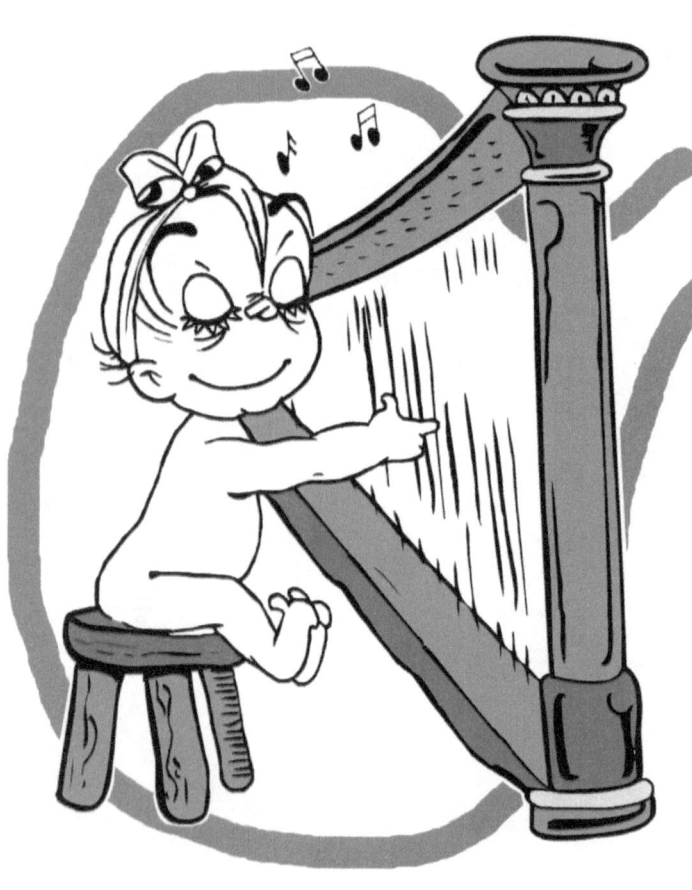

WITH A LOT OF PRACTICE MY
HARP MUSIC WILL LIFT YOUR SPIRITS
AND TOUCH YOUR SOUL

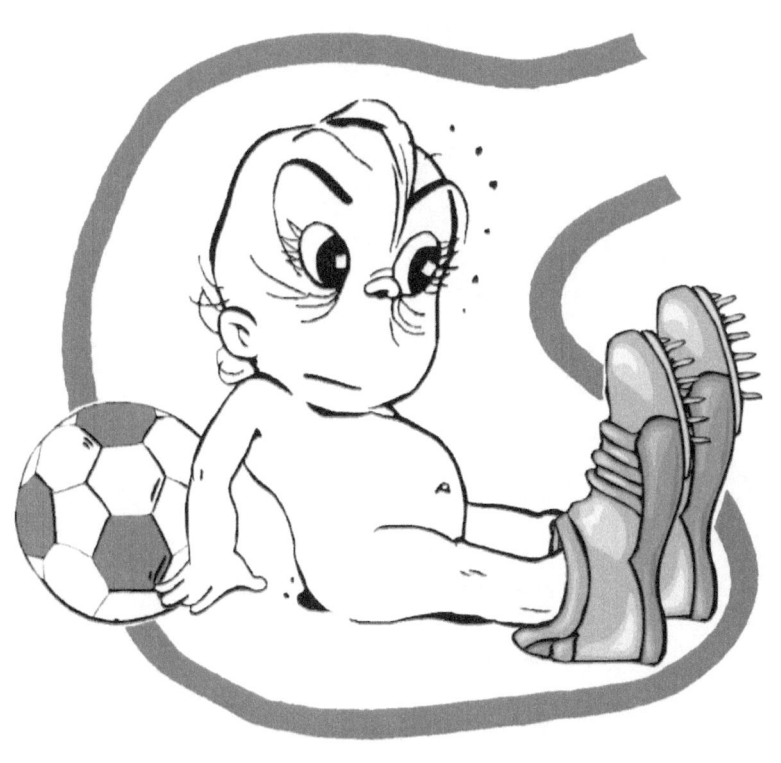

I GUESS I'LL BE WAITING AWHILE
BEFORE I CAN PLAY SOCCER.
(OR IS IT CALLED "FOOTBALL"?)

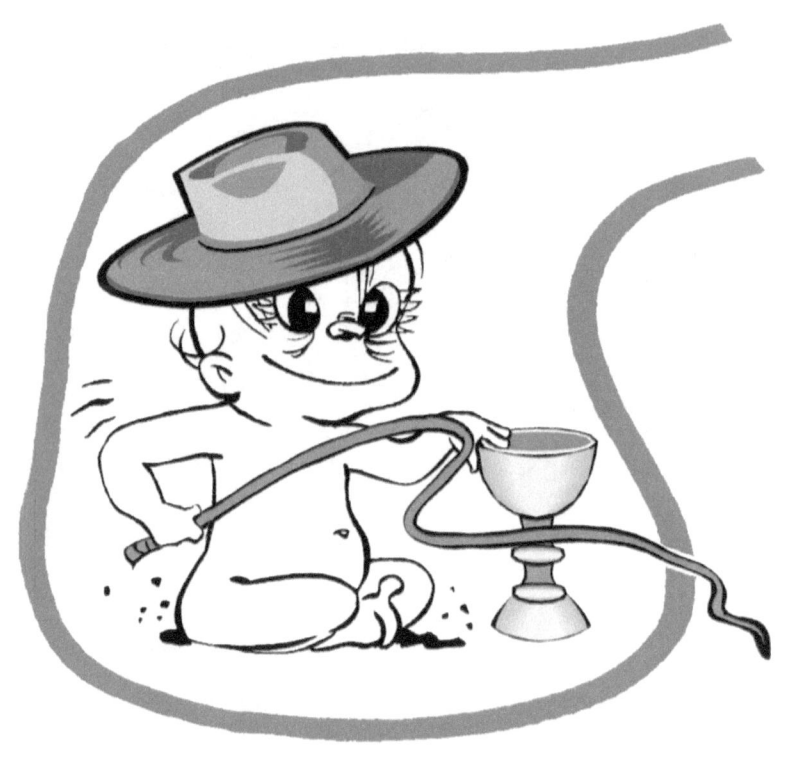

LOOK OUT INDY ... HERE I COME !
WE'LL FIND THE ARK !

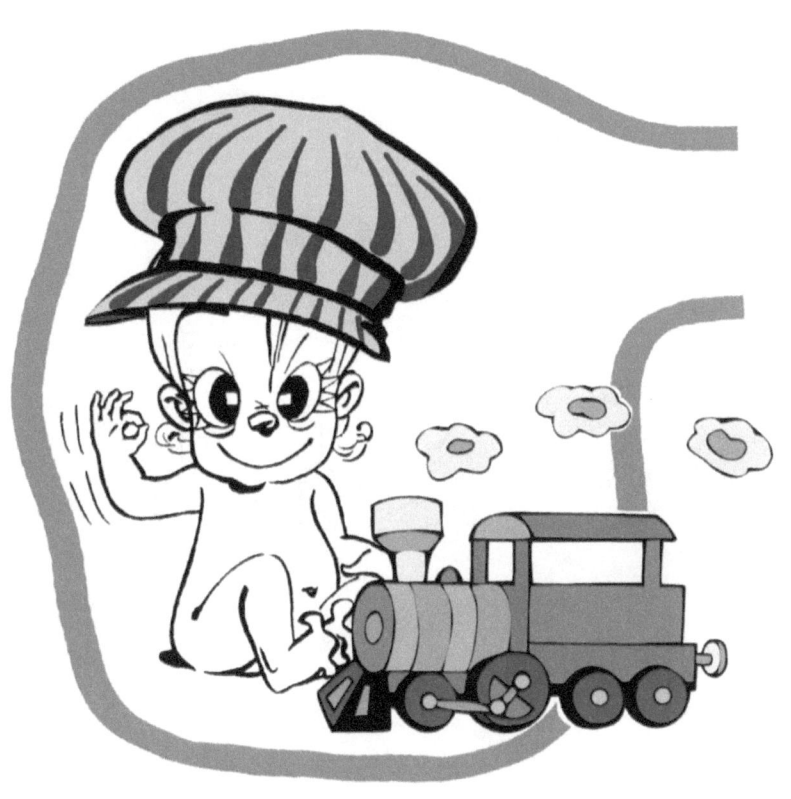

POP ALREADY PROMISED
ME A MODEL RAILROAD!

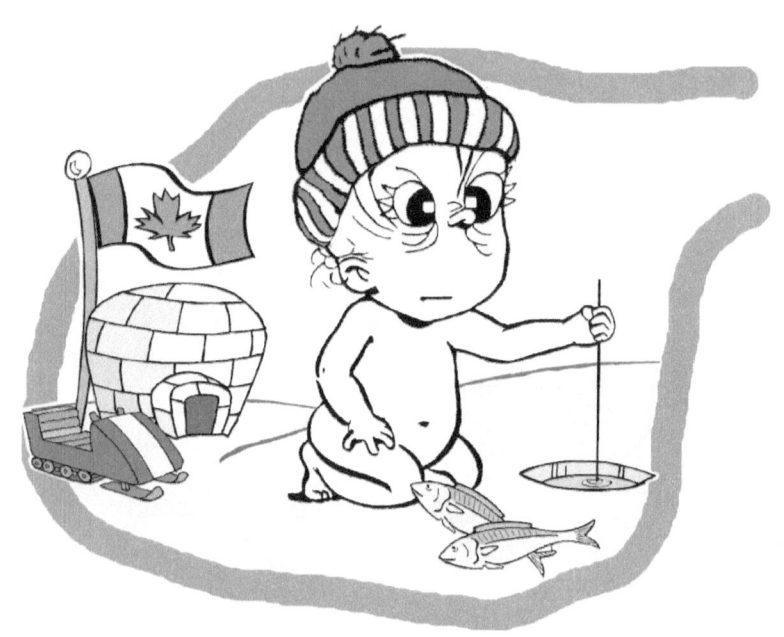

I THOUGHT FISHING OFF A PIER
WAS BAD. THIS IS JUST
PLAIN CRAZY ...
ICE FISHING ... BAH !

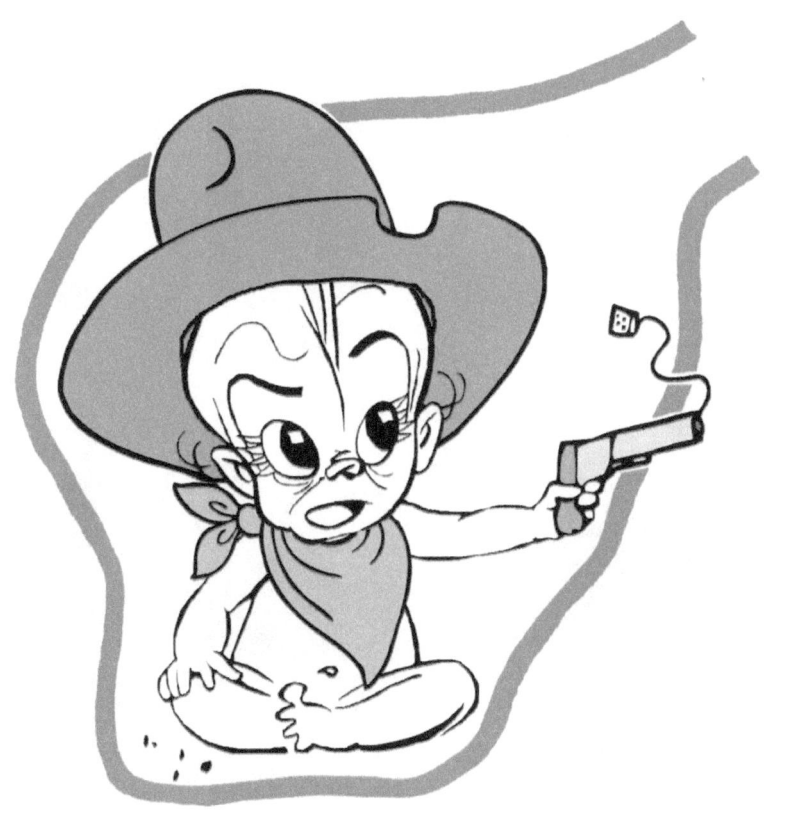

AWRIGHT .. WHO'S THE DADGUM
VARMINT WHO STOLE MY BOOTS?

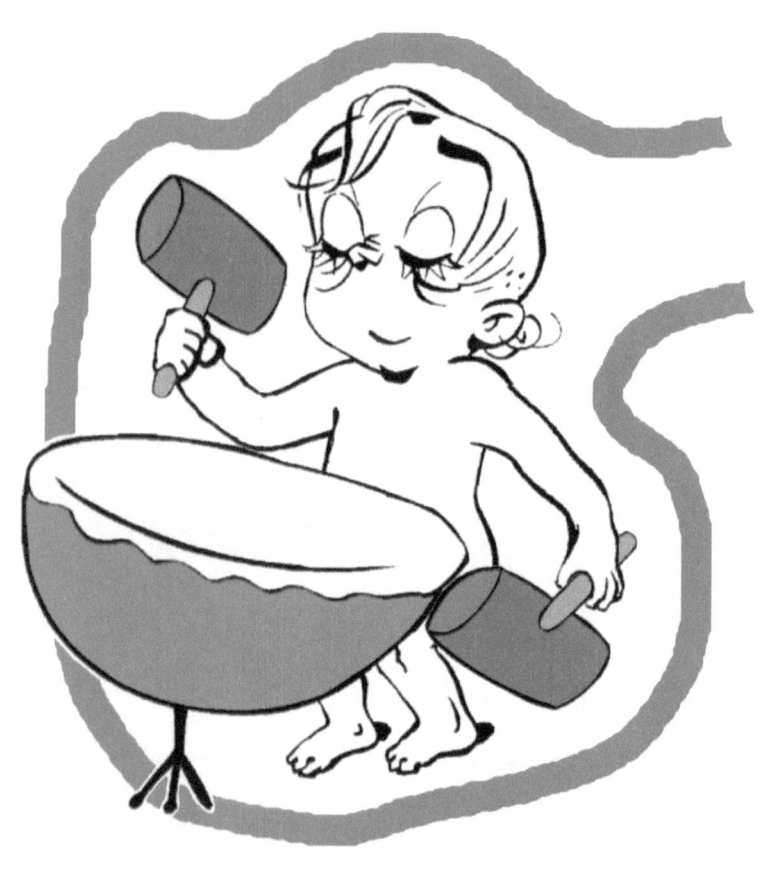

WHEN YOU'RE THE DRUMMER, THE
TEMPO IS WHATEVER <u>YOU</u> SAY IT IS!

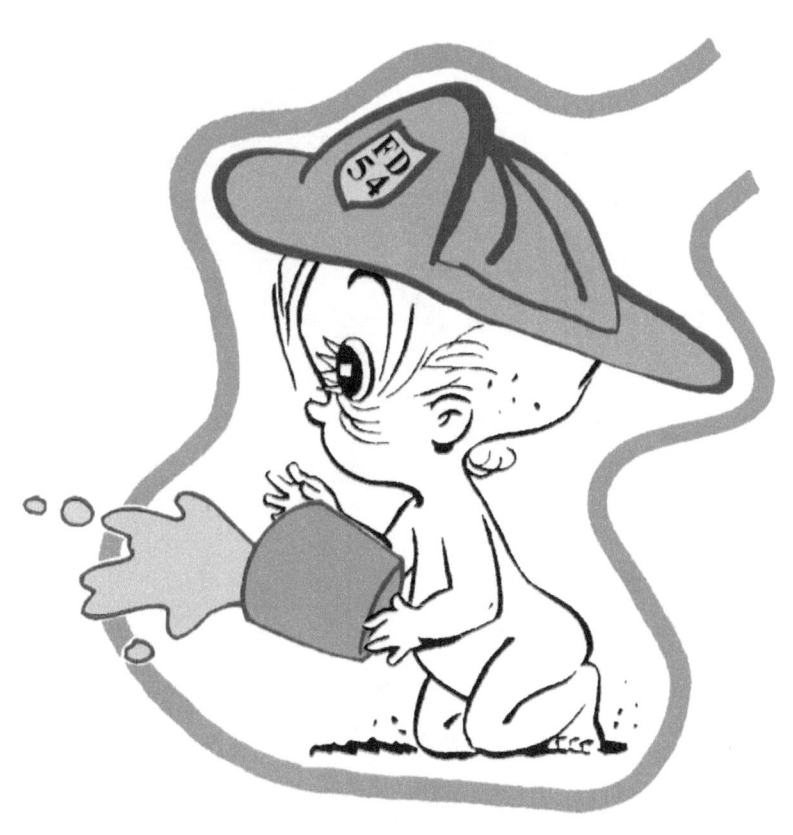

GEE, I HOPE I CAN BE A
FIRST RESPONDER SOMEDAY !

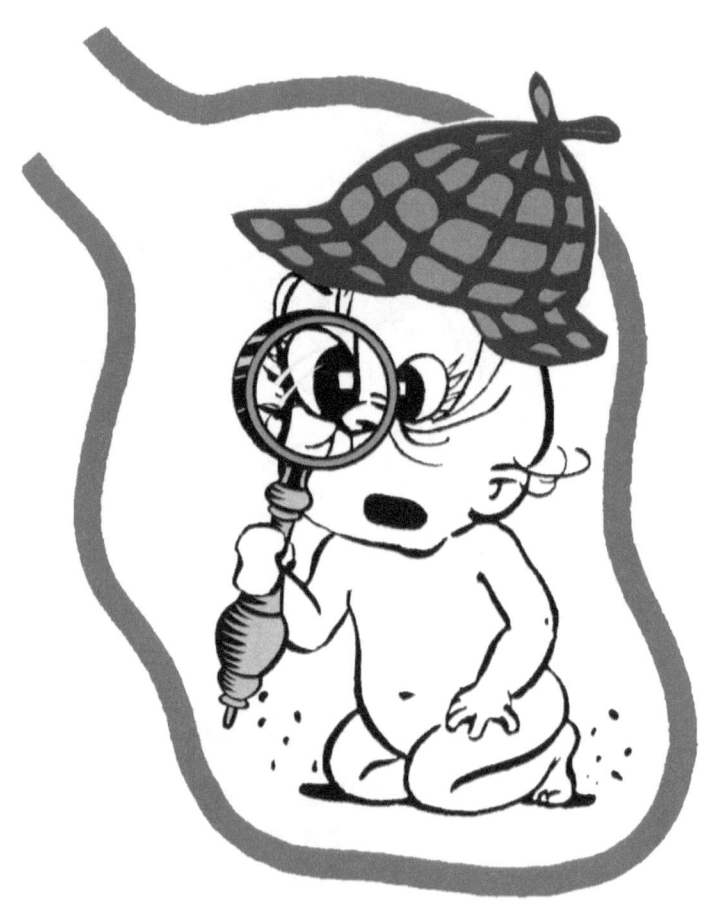

LET'S SEE ... SHALL I CHECK OUT
THE PRESIDENT OR THE
SPEAKER OF THE HOUSE?

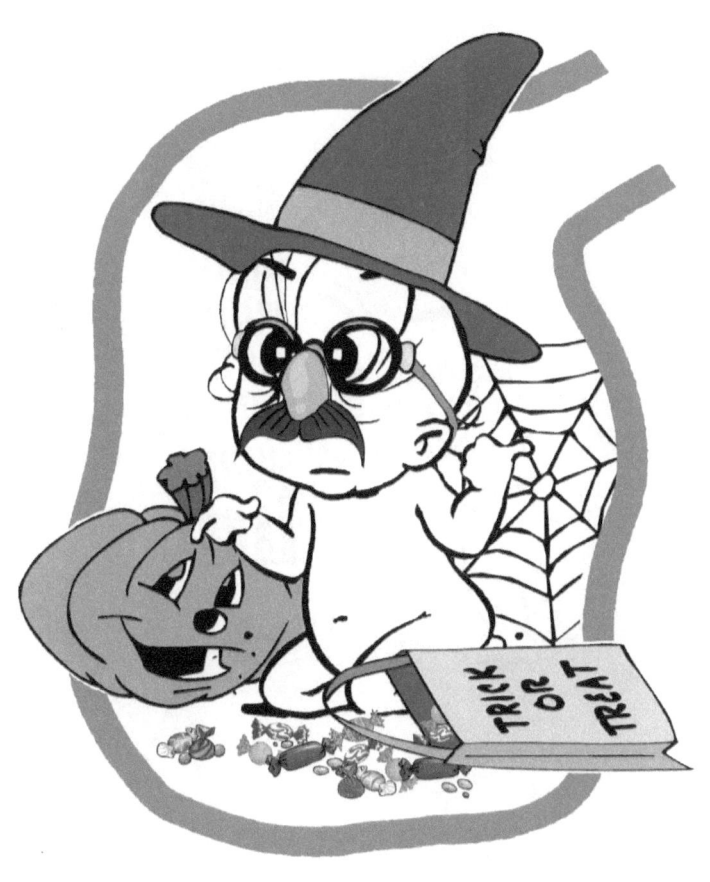

UH, MA... I CAN'T SEE THE
SPIDER WHAT MADE THIS WEB.
YOU KNOW WHERE IT WENT?

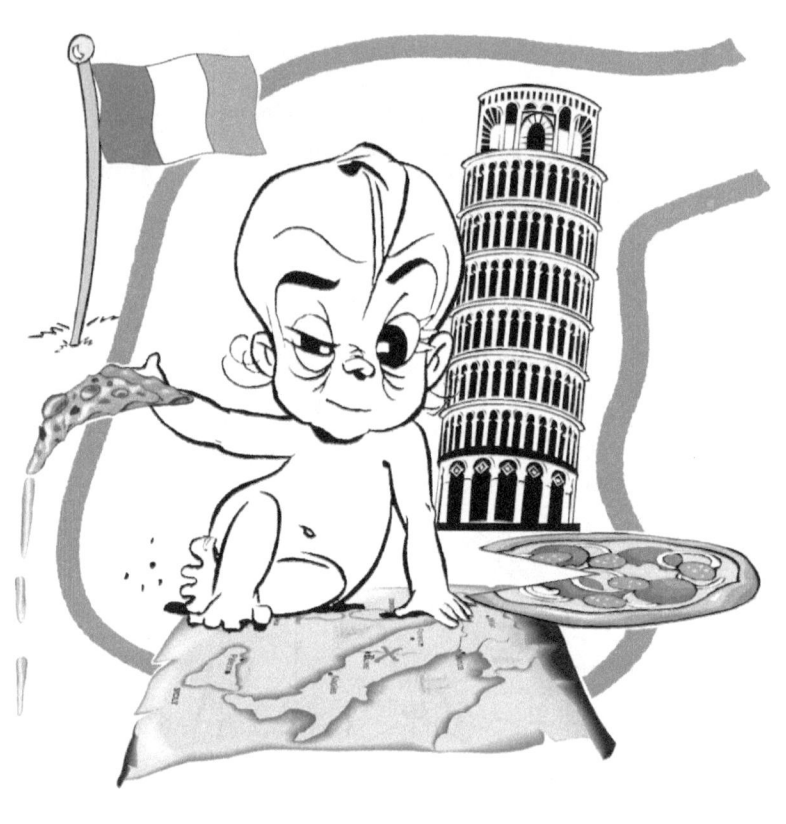

MA SAYS PIZZA IS THE BEST
THING TO COME OUT OF ITALY !

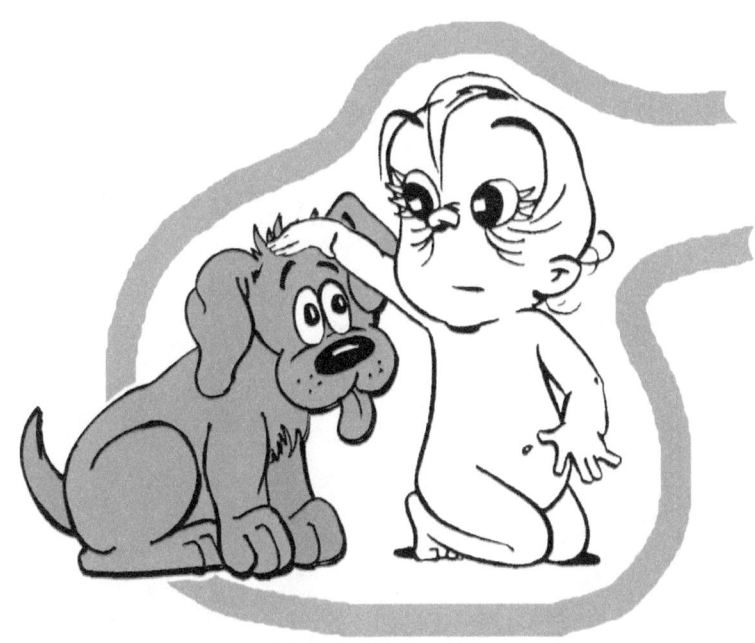

YOU CAN'T BE REAL !!
HOW'D YOU EVEN GET IN HERE?

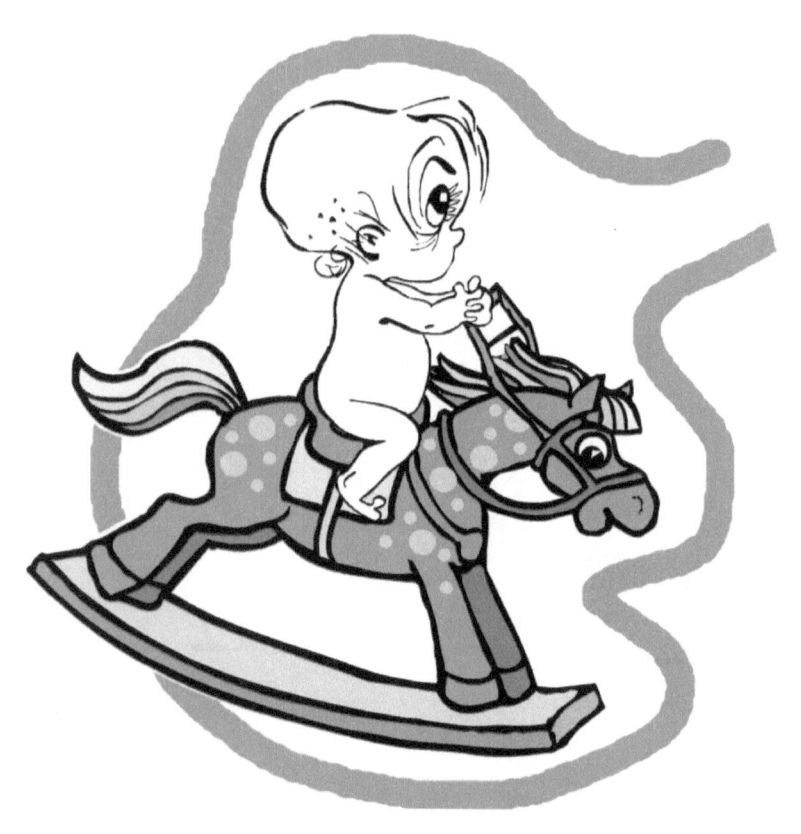

I SURE HOPE I'LL HAVE A
PONY ON THE OUTSIDE !

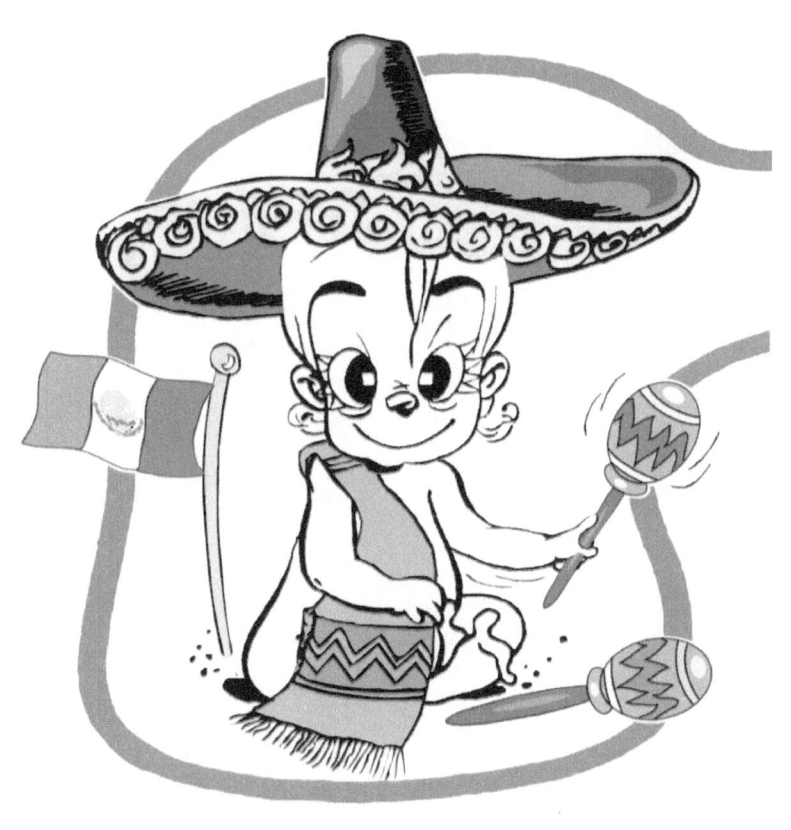

MA SAYS MEXICAN MUSIC MAKES
HER WANT TO DANCE.
ME TOO !

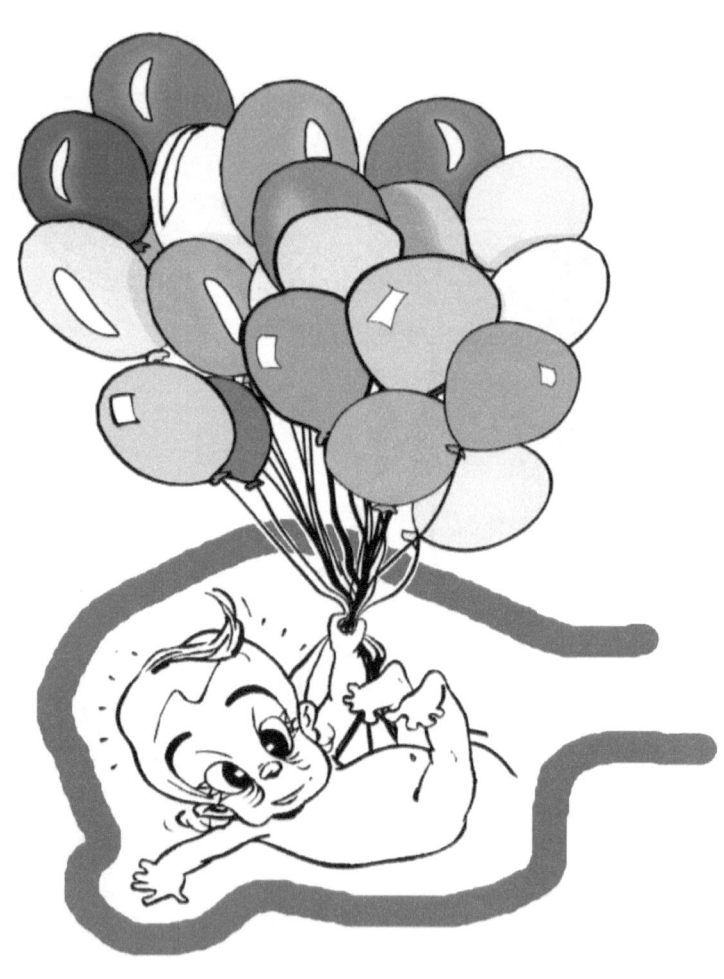

HEY, MA ... DOES THIS LIGHTEN YOUR
LOAD UNTIL I GET OUTTA HERE??

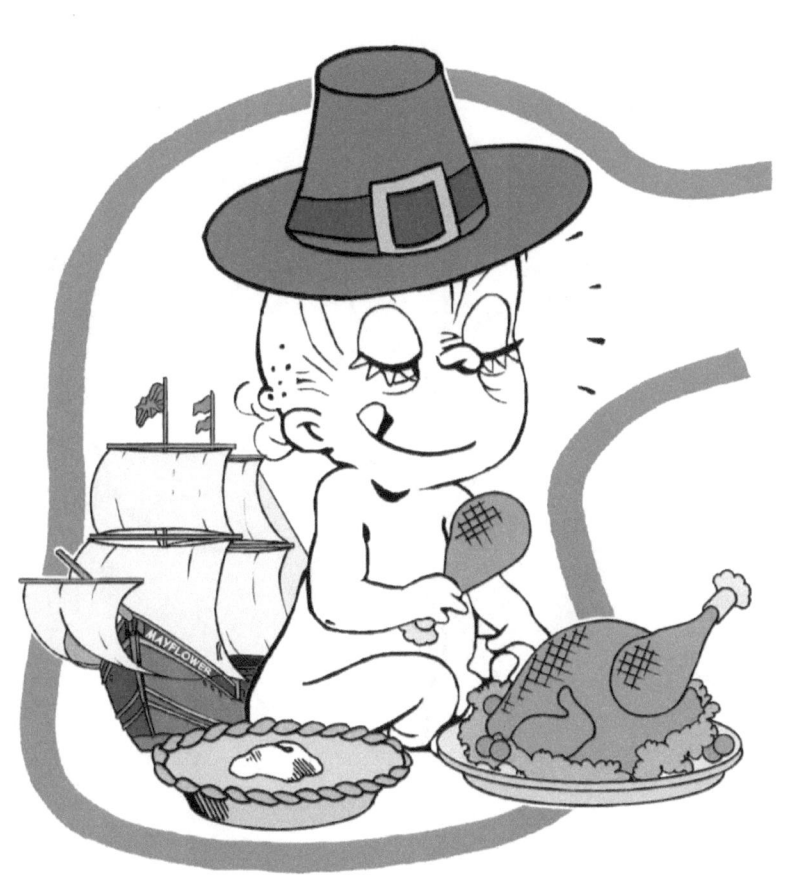

I THINK I'M GONNA LIKE
HOLIDAYS IF THE FOOD'S
ALWAYS THIS GOOD!

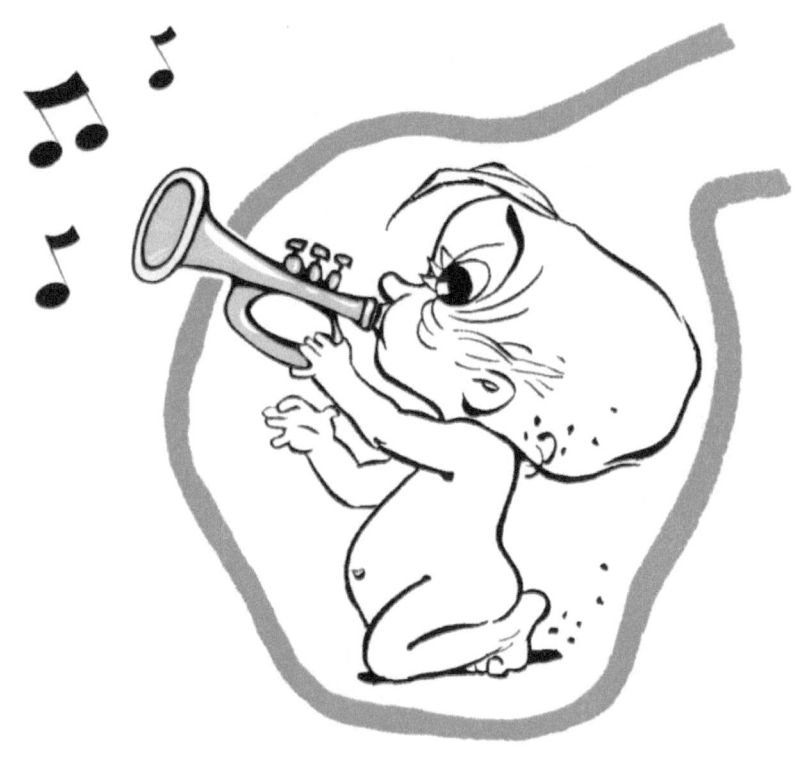

I'M THE BOOGIE-WOOGIE
BUGLE BOY !

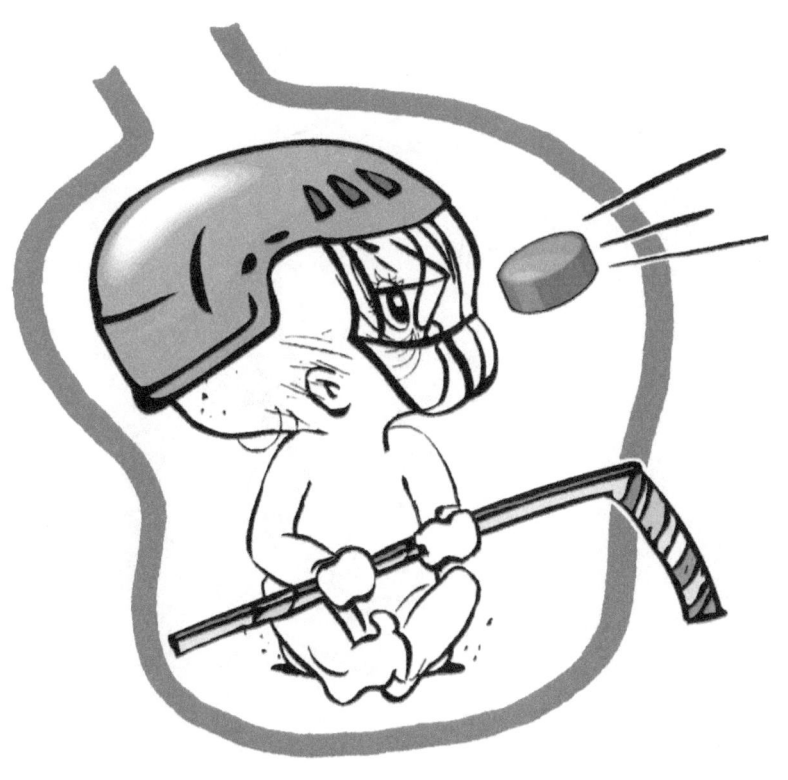

UH ... THESE FACEGUARDS WERE MADE
BY THE LOWEST BIDDER, WEREN'T THEY?
(THIS IS GONNA HURT ...)

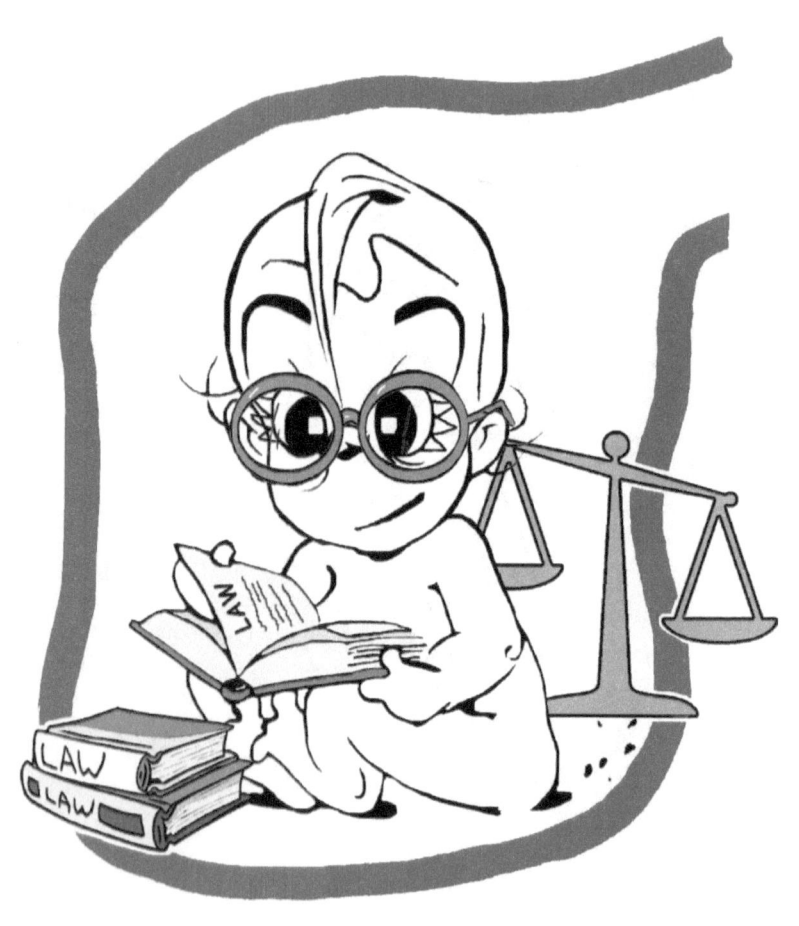

I SURE HOPE THERE'S ROOM
FOR ONE MORE LAWYER!

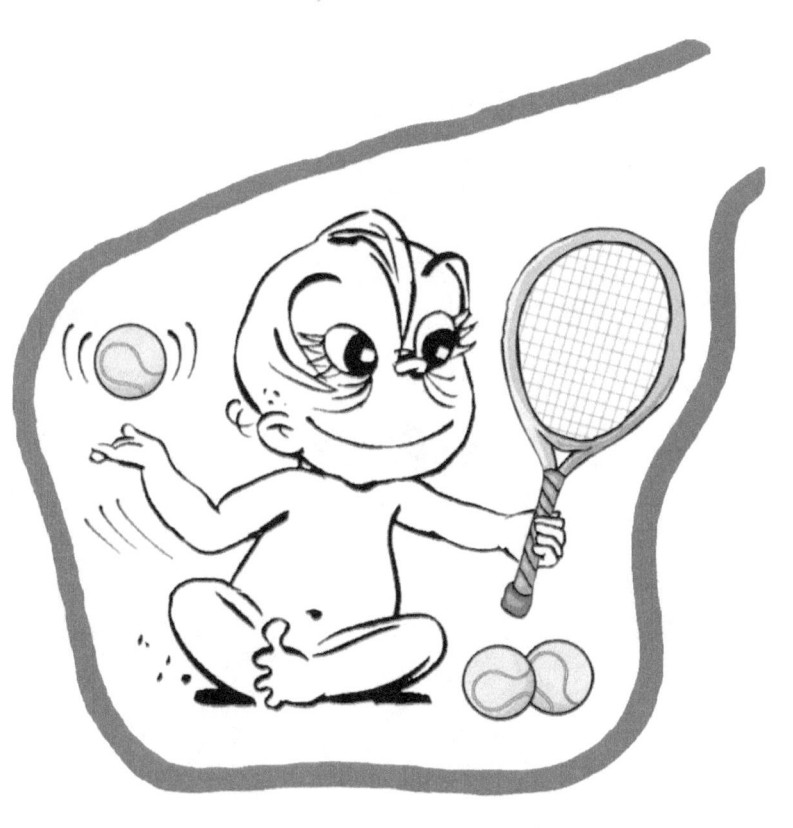

WIMBLEDON ...
HERE I COME !!

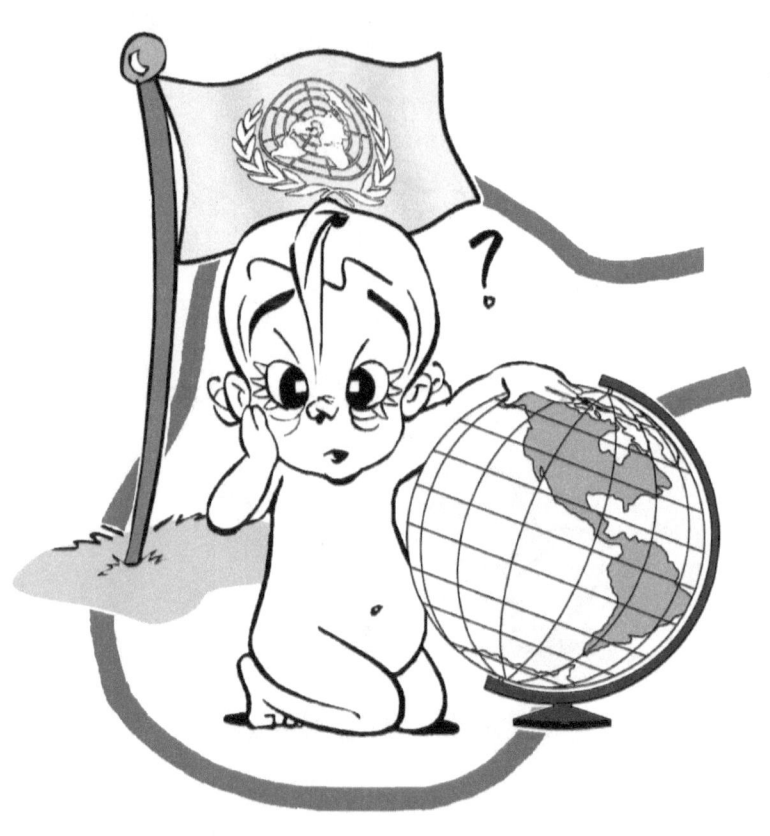

HOW DO YOU GET THE U.N.
TO PASS A RESOLUTION FOR A
WORLD-WIDE CEASE FIRE ?

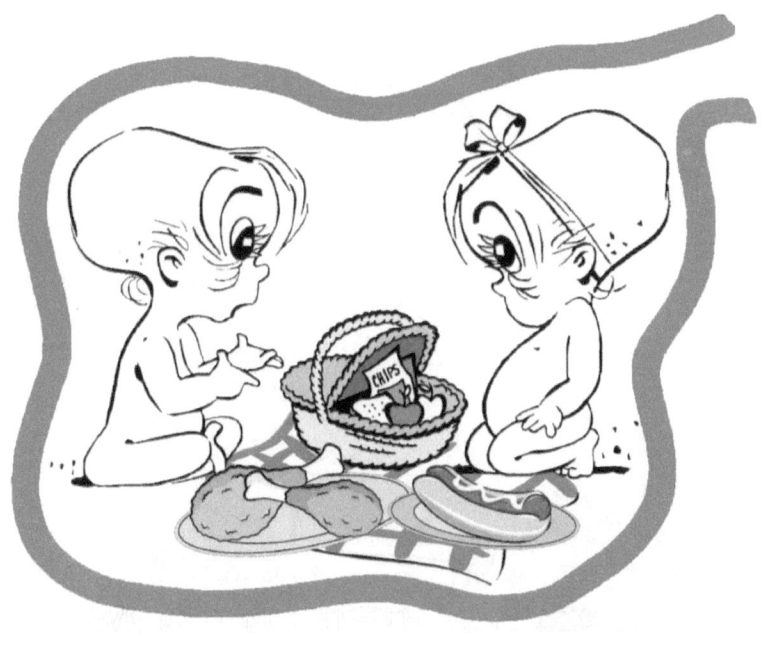

WE GOT NO TEETH YET, SIS ...
HOW WE GONNA EAT THIS STUFF?

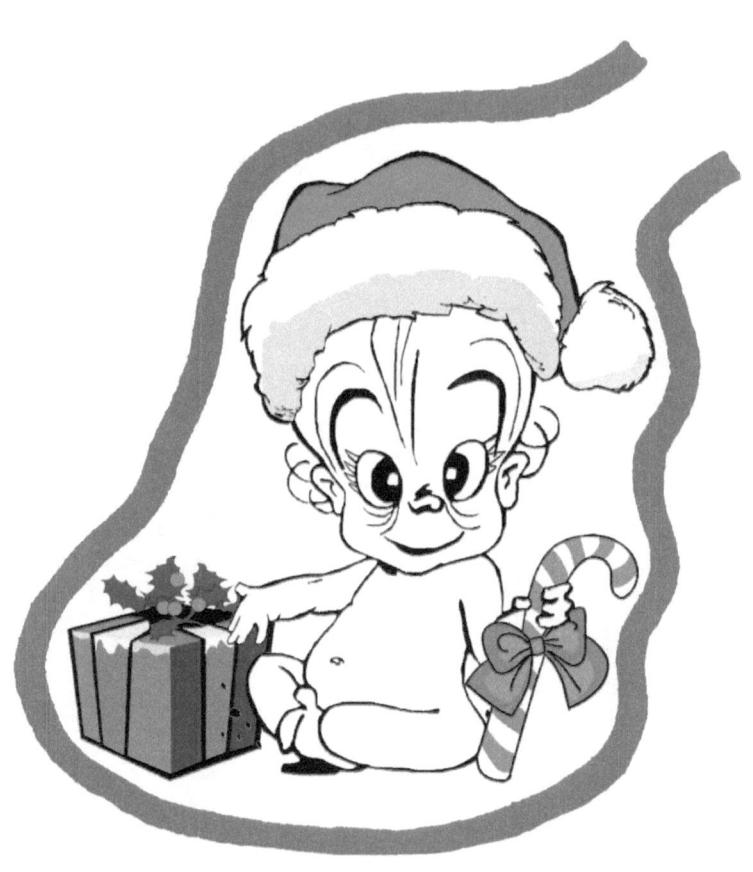

WOW, MOM & POP ARE TALKIN'
ABOUT CHRISTMAS ..
I'M GONNA LIKE THIS HOLIDAY !

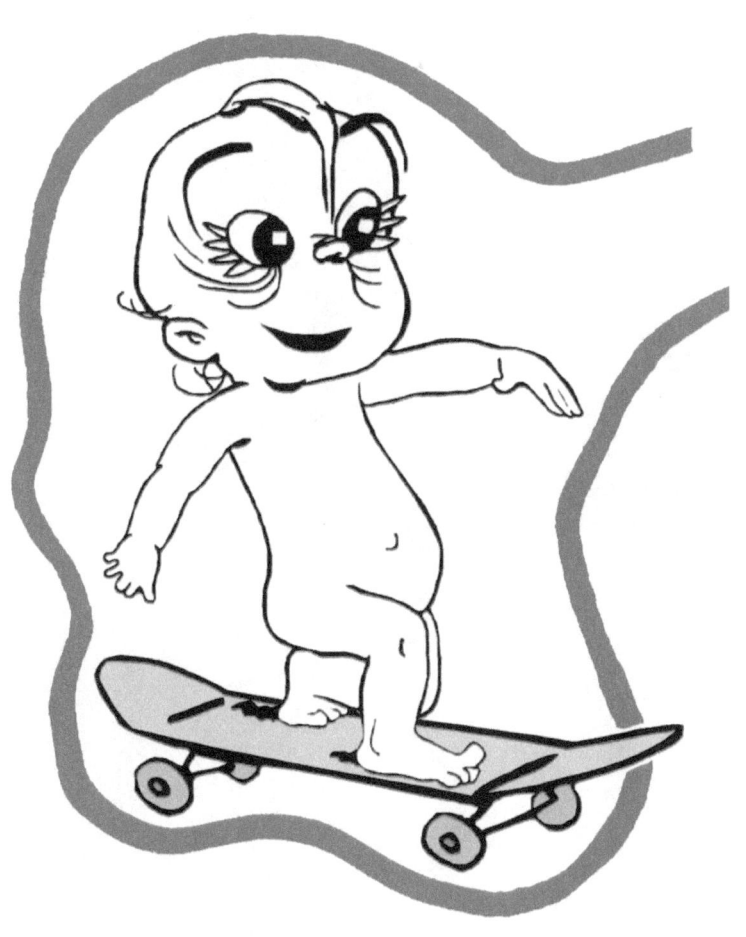

I THINK I'M READY TO
TRY A WHEELIE !

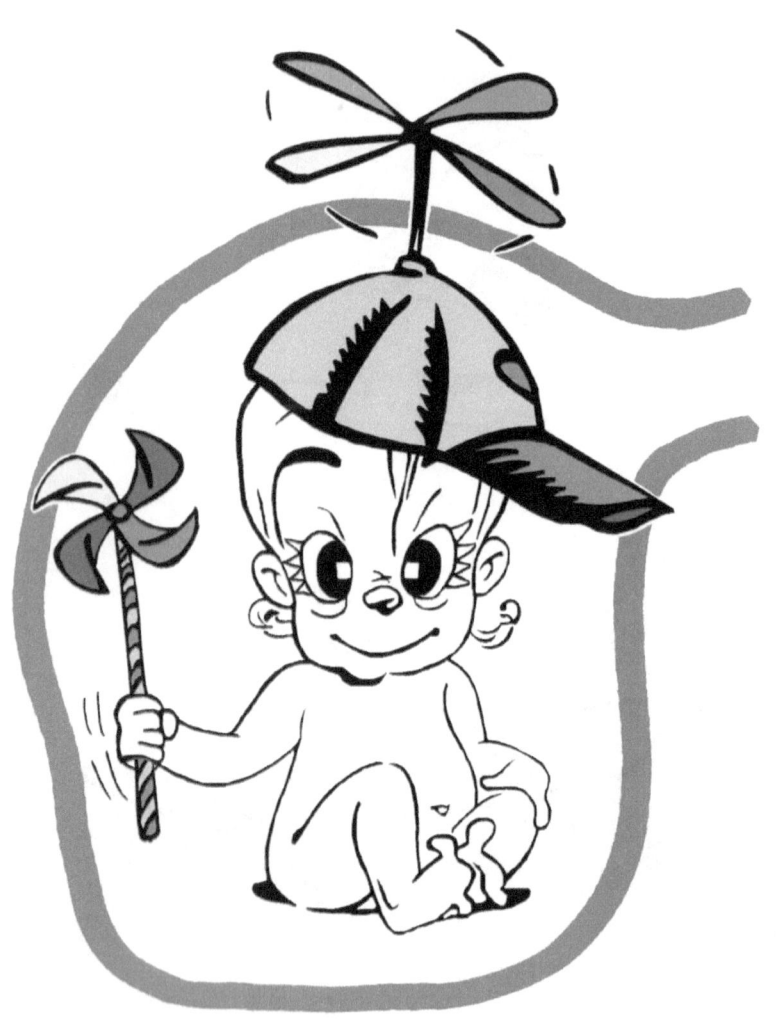

WITH <u>THIS</u> HAT, YOU CAN'T
REALLY TAKE ME <u>TOO</u> SERIOUS !

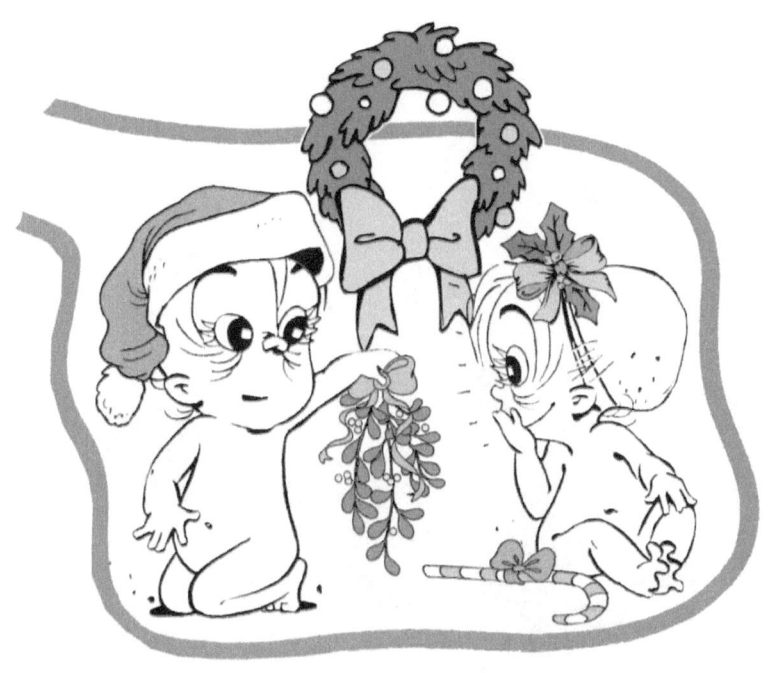

I DUNNO WHAT IT'S FOR ... MA
KEEPS TRYIN' TO GET POP
TO STAND UNDER IT !

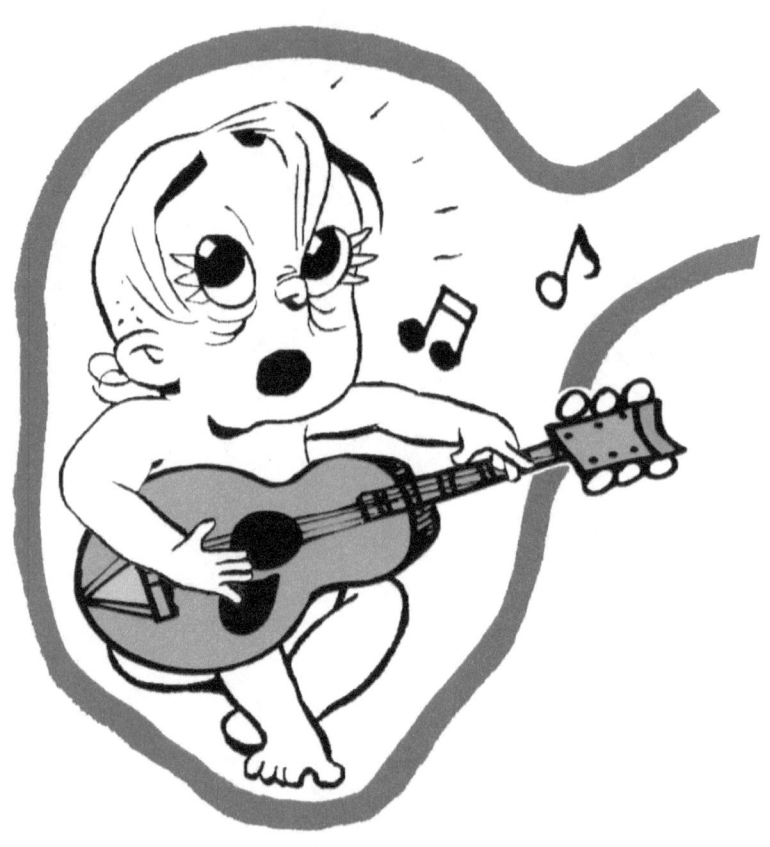

I'M READY FOR MY
"IDOL" AUDITION !

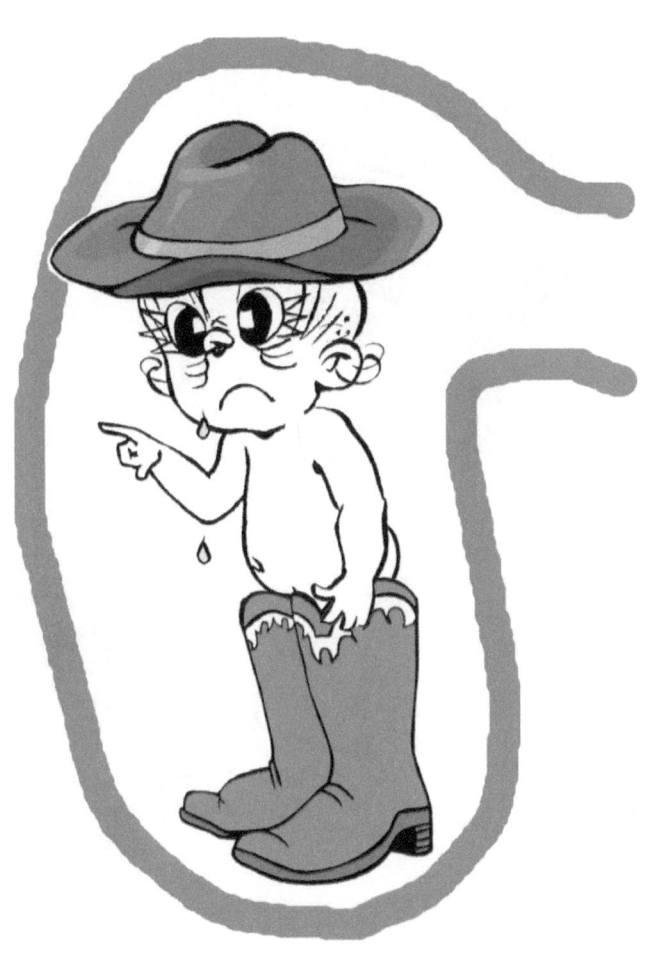

I TOL' YA POP'S BOOTS
WOULD BE TOO BIG !

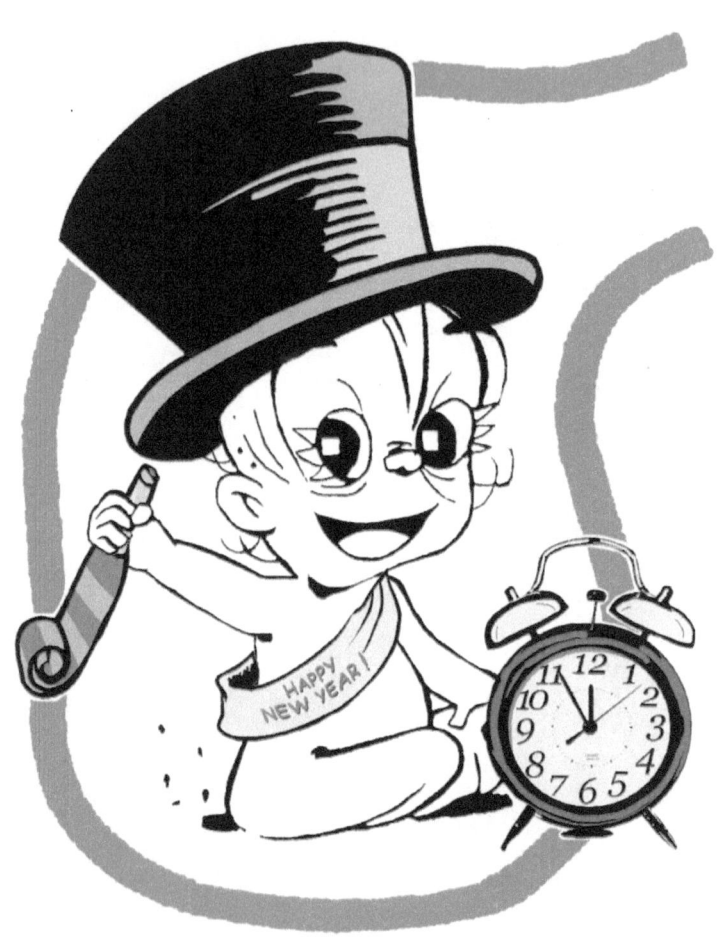

WOO, WOO!! I HEAR THERE'S A
BIG PARTY FOR NEW YEAR'S -
I CAN'T WAIT !

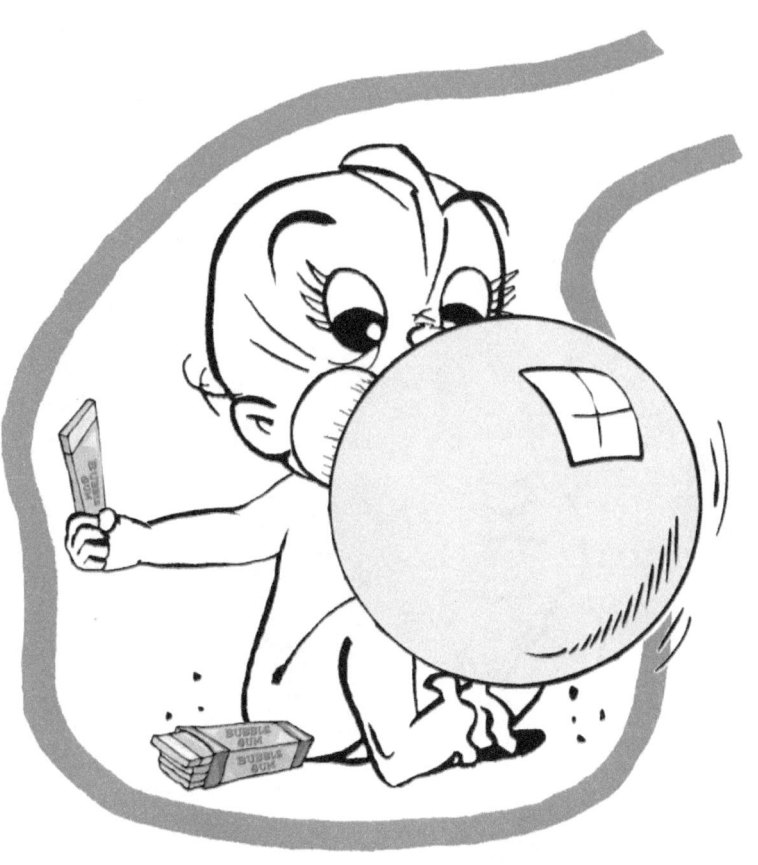

HEY, MA ...
I THINK I MIGHT FART ...

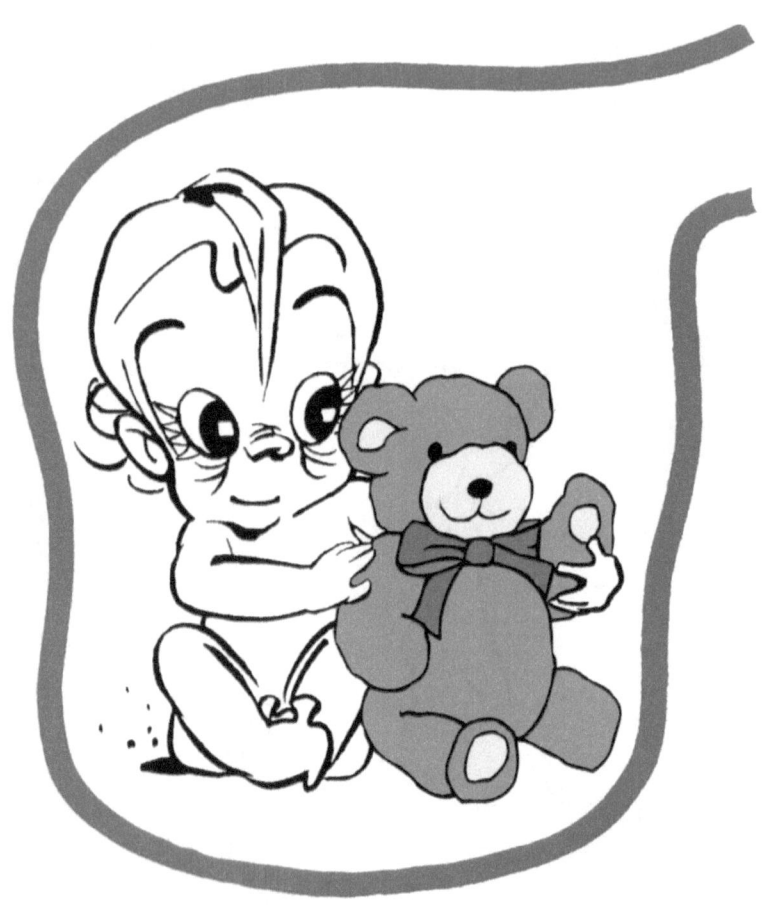

WONDER IF MOM WILL BE SURPRISED
IF I SHOW UP WITH A TEDDY BEAR?

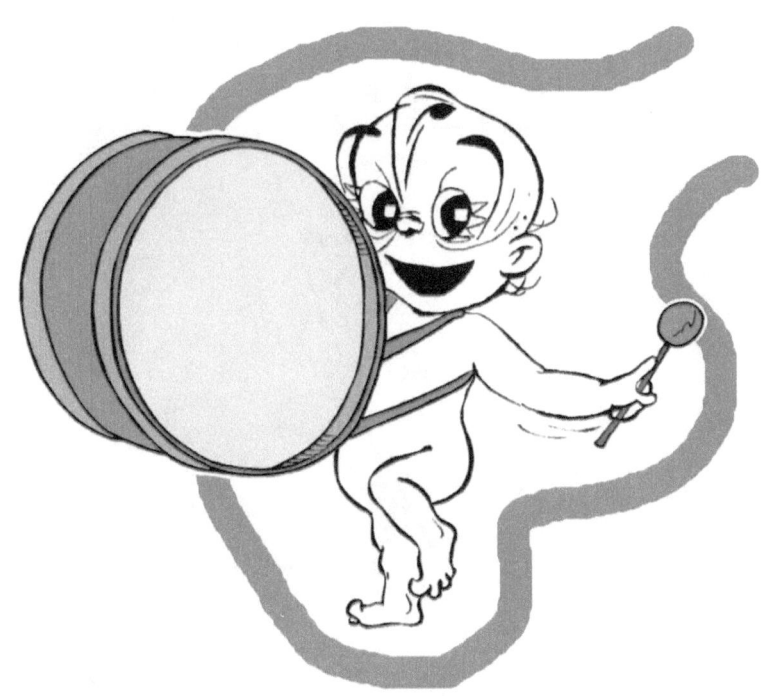

HEH, HEH ... WAIT 'TIL POP
HEARS THIS !!

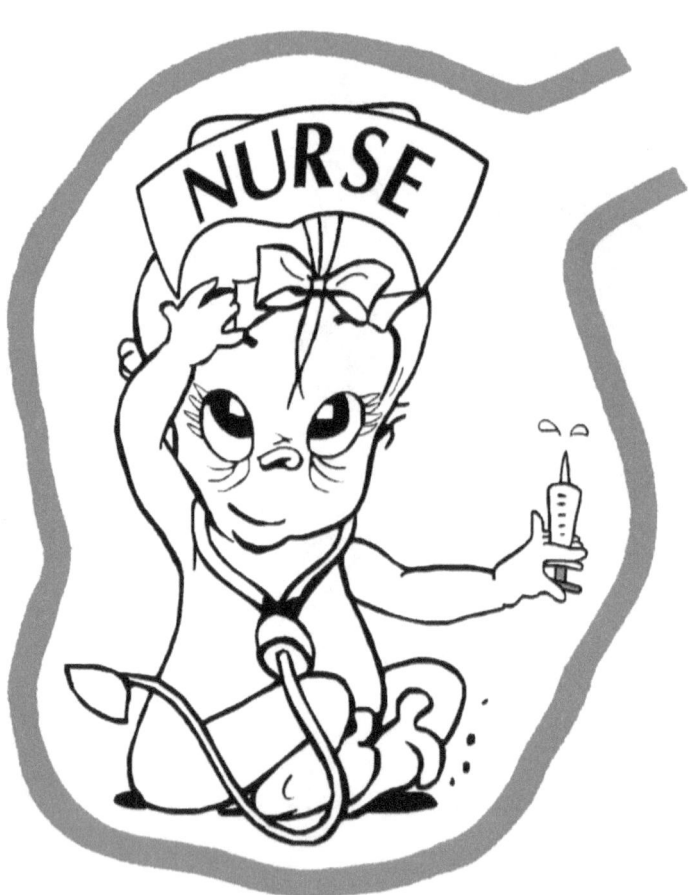

I'LL GIVE SHOTS & THEN EXPLAIN
WHAT THE DOCTOR SAID

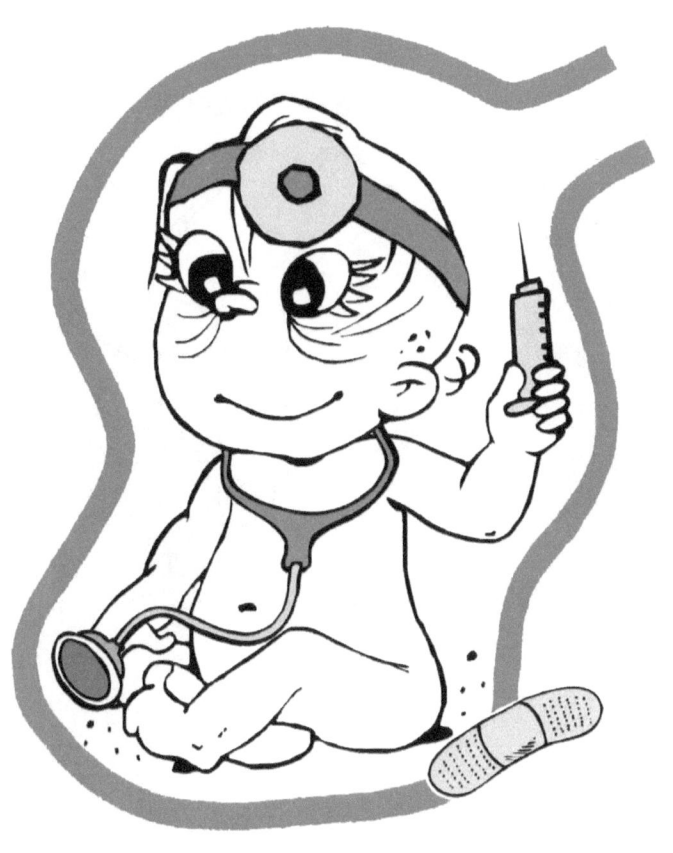

IS A FLU SHOT LIKE
INSTALLING
VIRUS PROTECTION SOFTWARE?

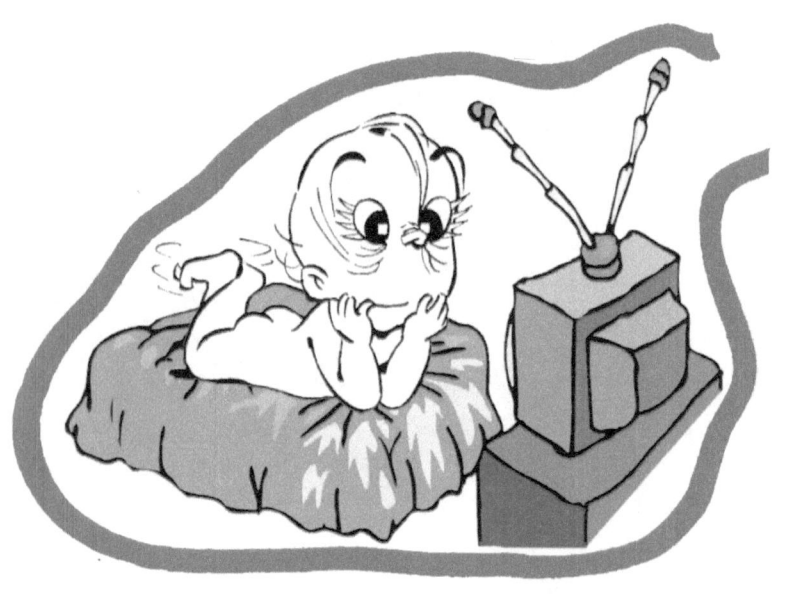

I WONDER IF THE RECEPTION IS
BETTER ON THE OUTSIDE ...

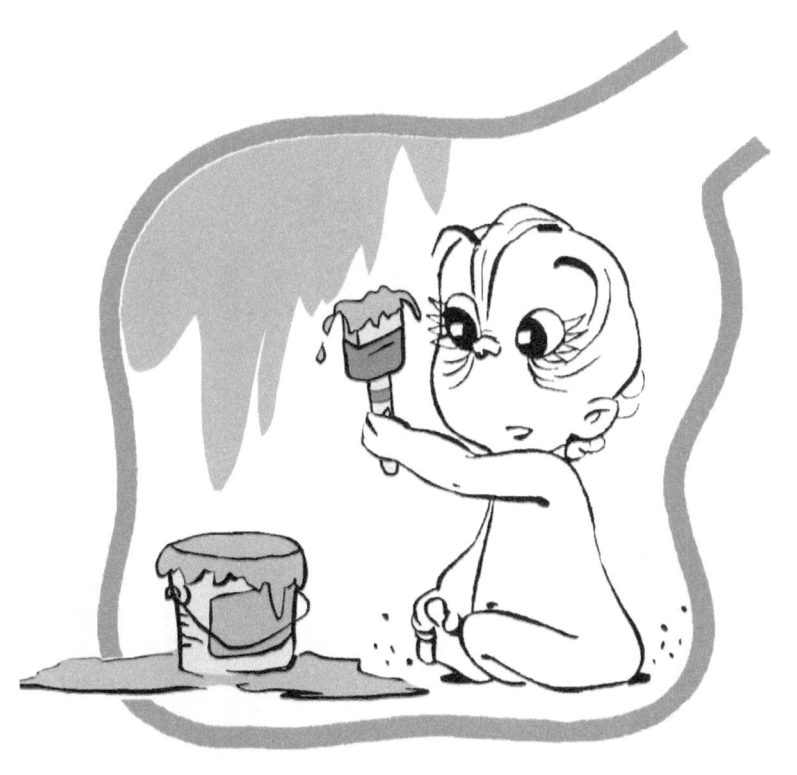

I THOUGHT I'D SPRUCE UP THE PLACE
WITH SOME PAINT
BEFORE THE NEXT TENANT GETS HERE!

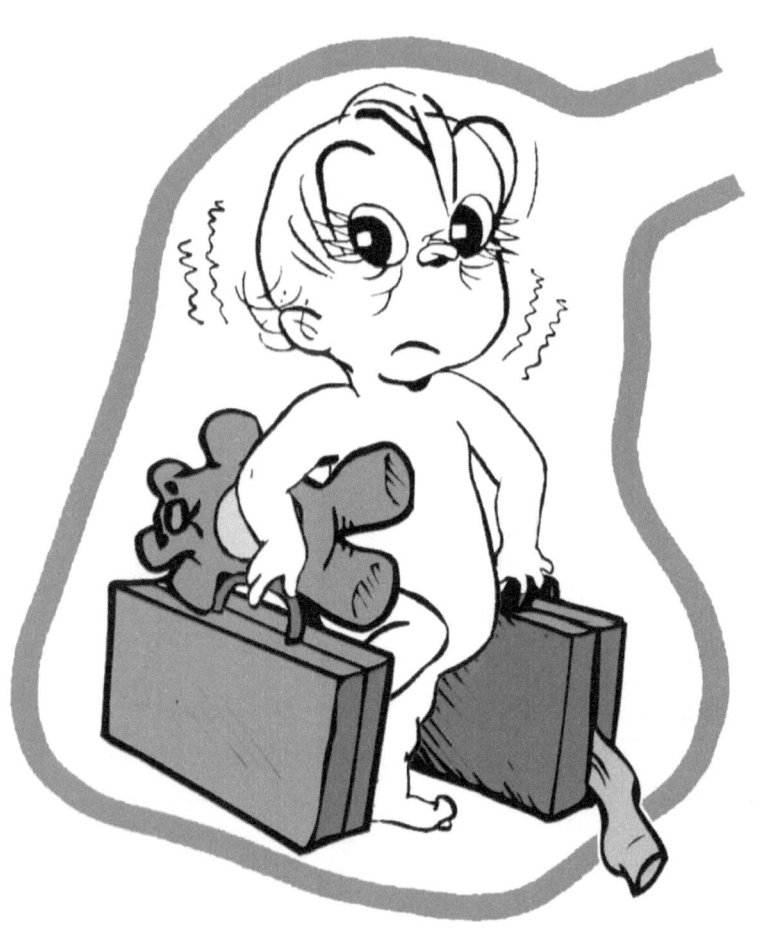

BAGS ARE PACKED, SO I'M READY.
GONNA MISS THIS PLACE !

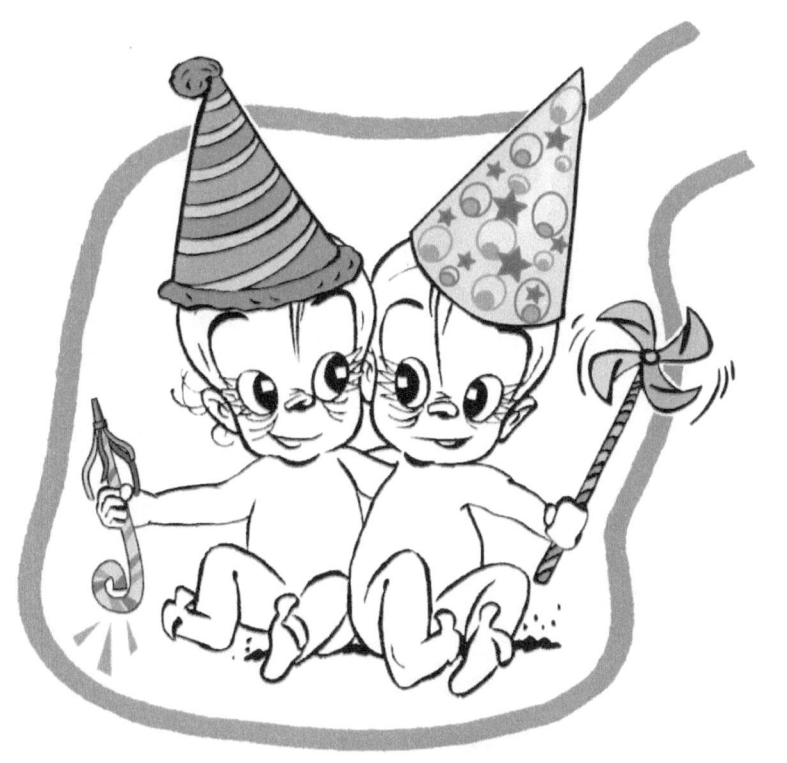

WE'RE READY FOR OUR
COMING OUT <u>PARTY</u> !

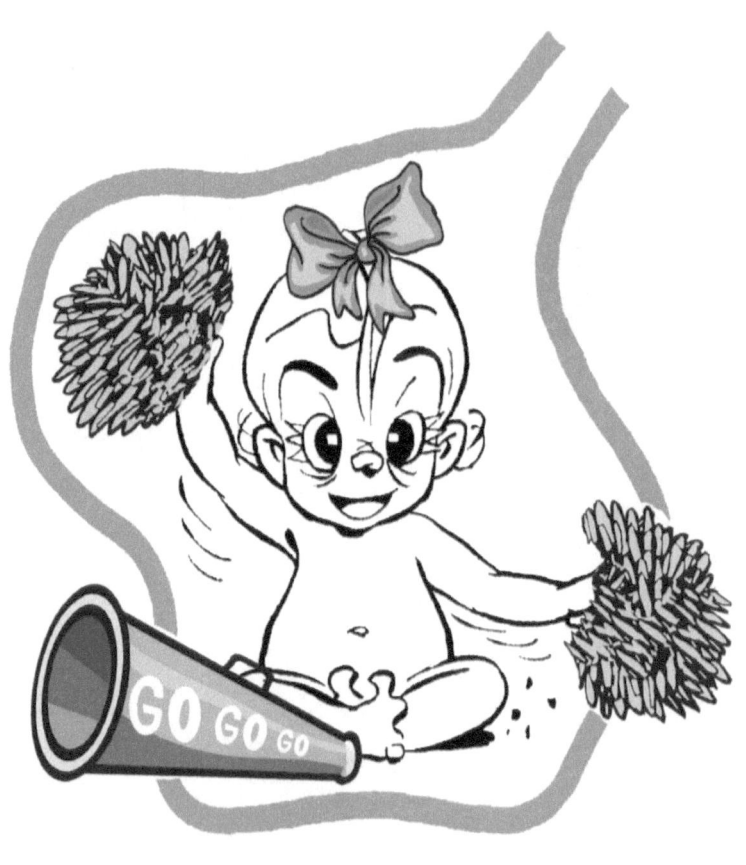

HIP, HIP, HOORAY!
TOMORROW'S MY BIRTHDAY!

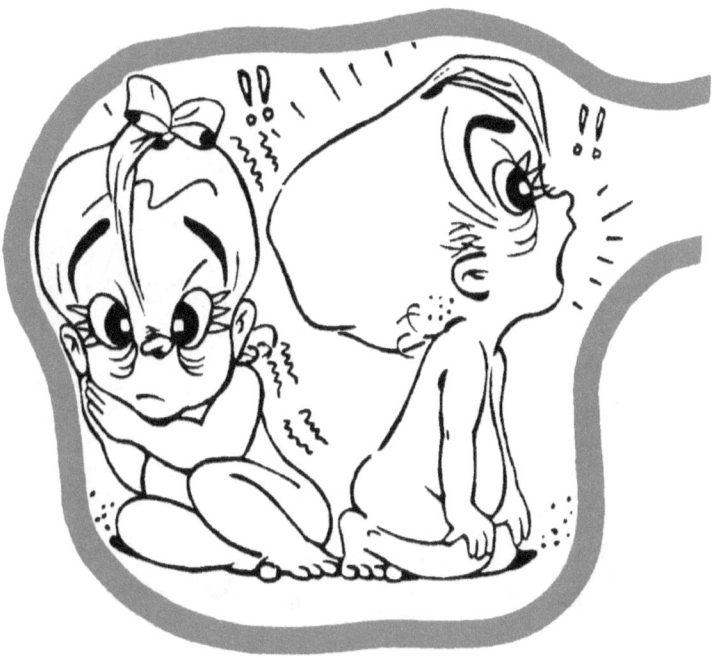

THIS IS A HELLUVA TIME TO BE CHECKING YOUR MEDICAL BOOK !

From *Eggbert Belly Laughs*

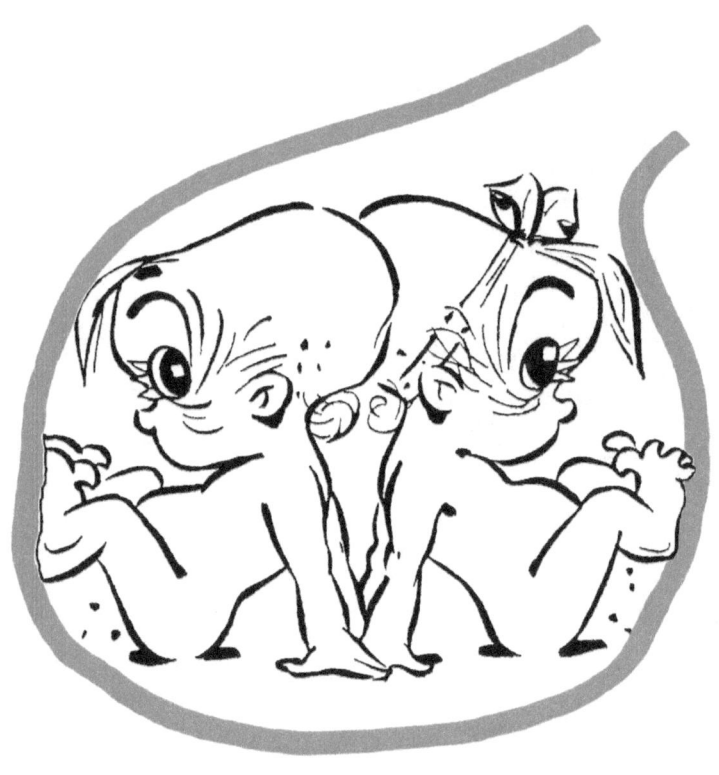

THE NEXT TIME ANYBODY
SAYS "PUSH" -- <u>SLUG</u> 'EM !

From: *Eggbert's Diary For A Lady In Waiting*

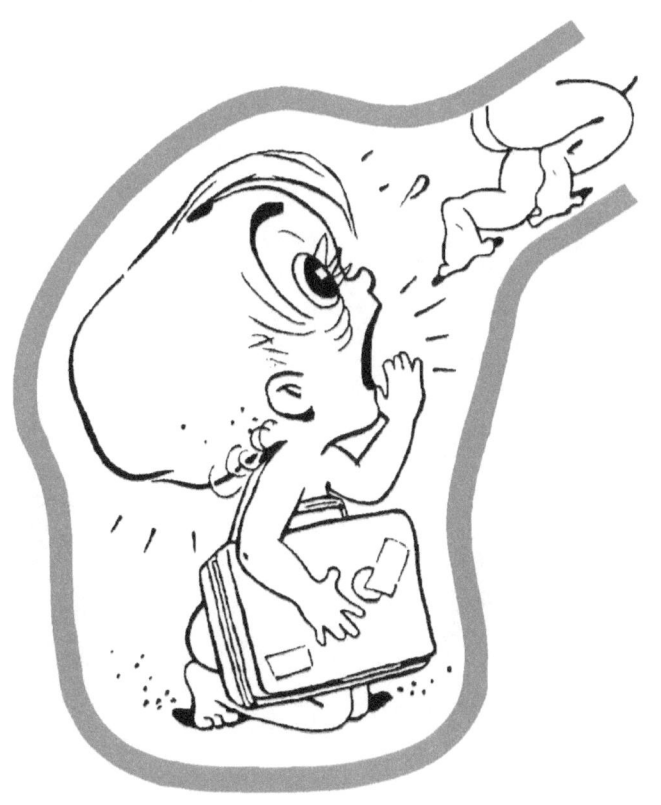

HEY ! KEEP THE HATCH OPEN !
MORE COMIN' !

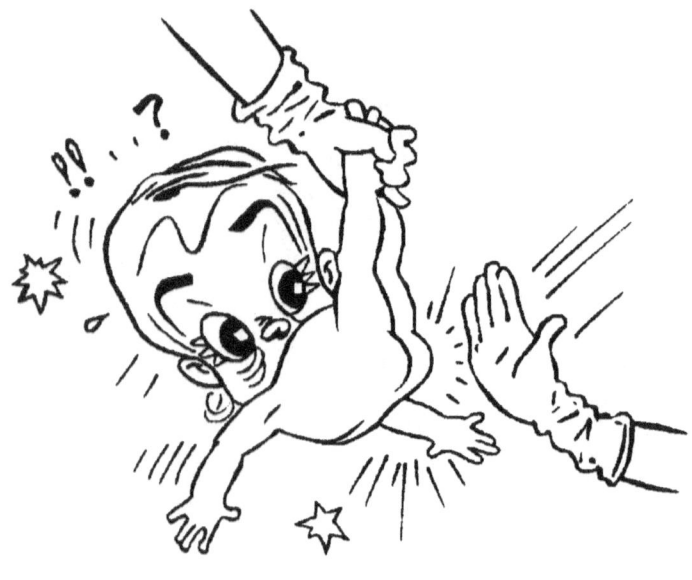

THIS IS A HELL OF A WAY
TO SPEND A SATURDAY AFTERNOON !

From *Eggbert Belly Laughs*

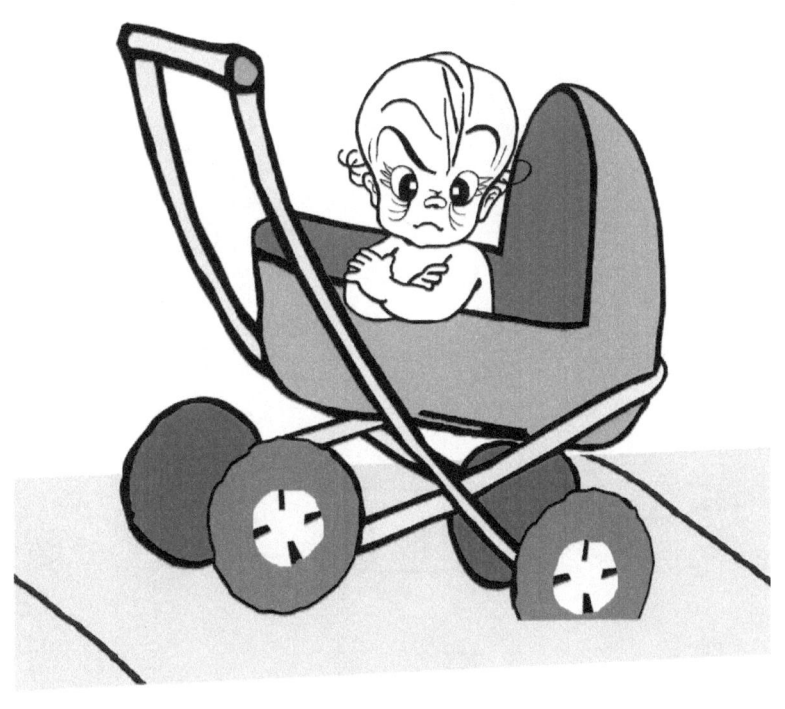

WELL THIS IS JUST GREAT. I'M FINALLY
BORN AND I GET A BUGGY WITH A
DEFECTIVE TIRE! C'MON POP ...
CAN'T YOU FIX IT?

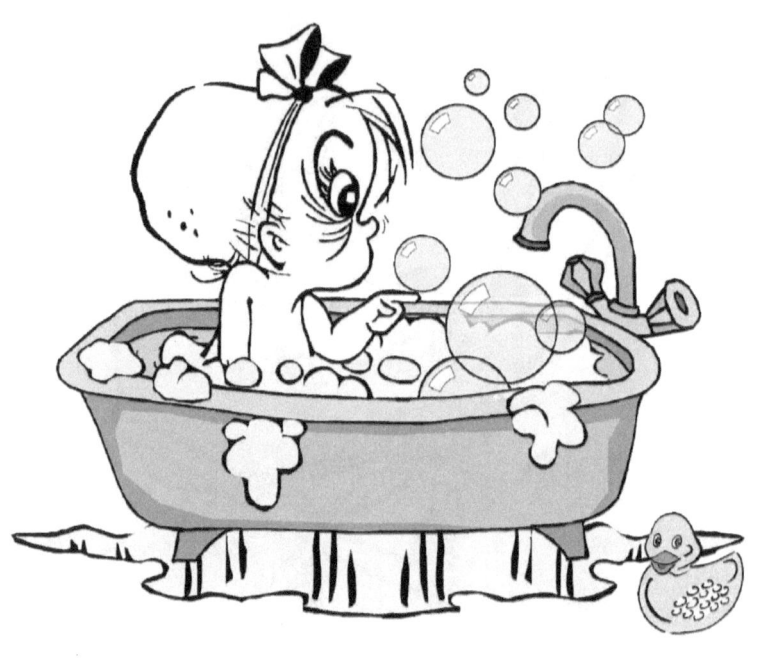

MUSTA BEEN THE BEANS ...
THESE BUBBLES SMELL FUNNY !

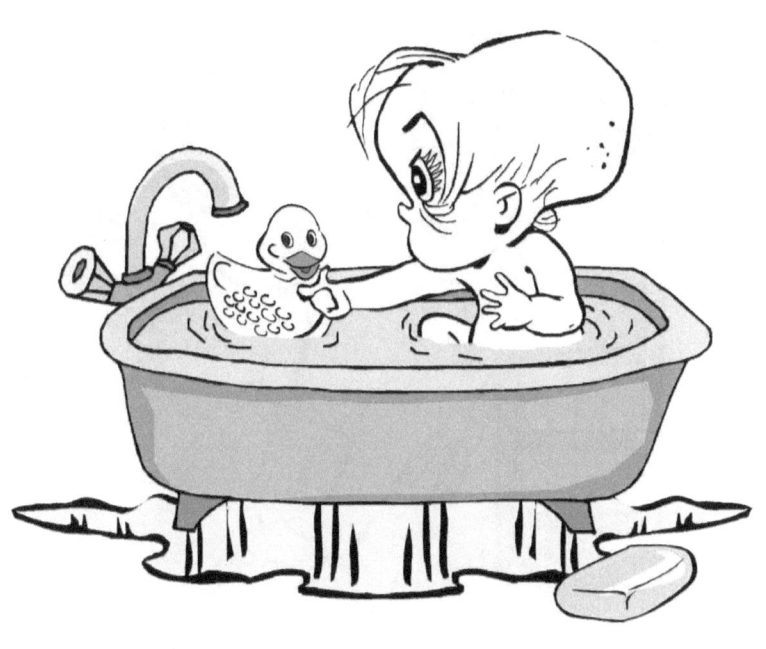

SHE GETS BUBBLES ...
ALL I GET IS A DUMB DUCKY !

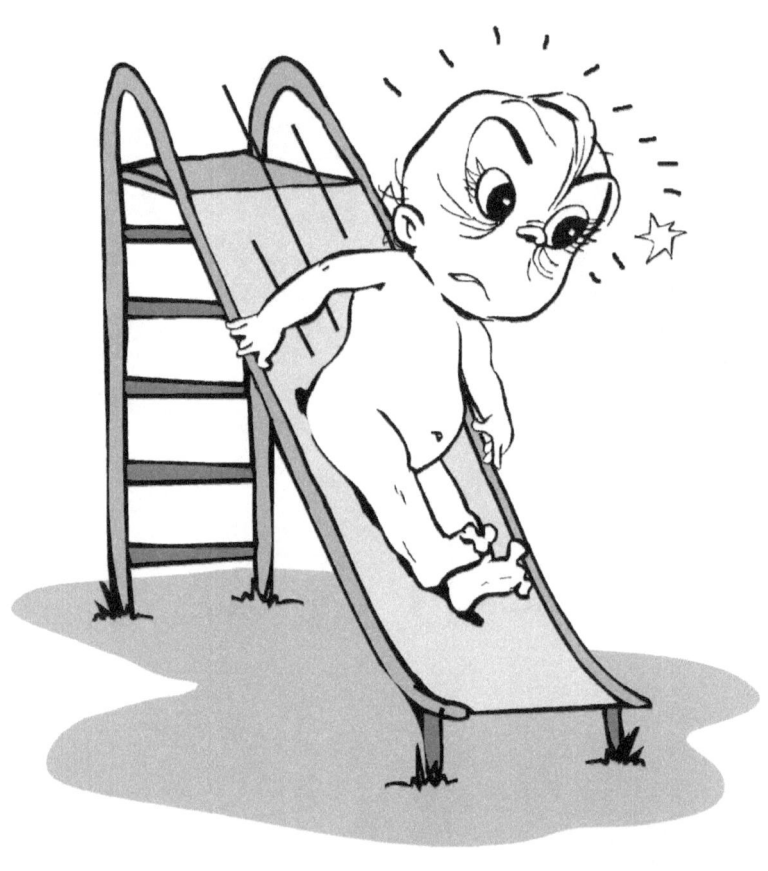

WOW, THE SUN MADE THIS
REALLY HOT !

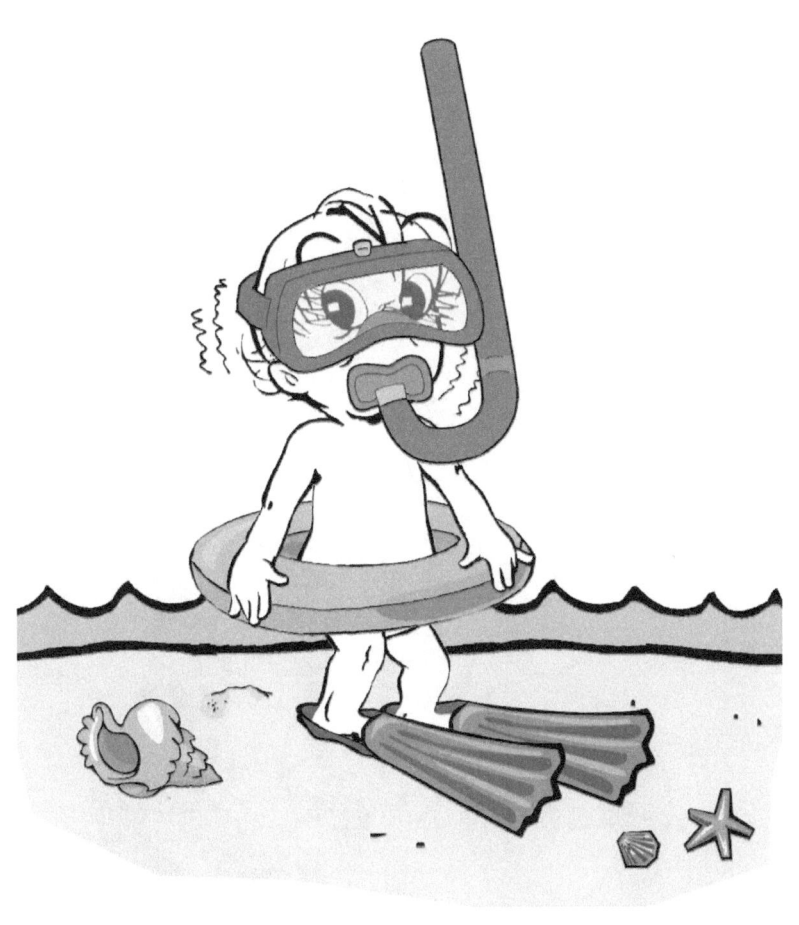

OKAY . . . <u>NOW</u> WHAT ?

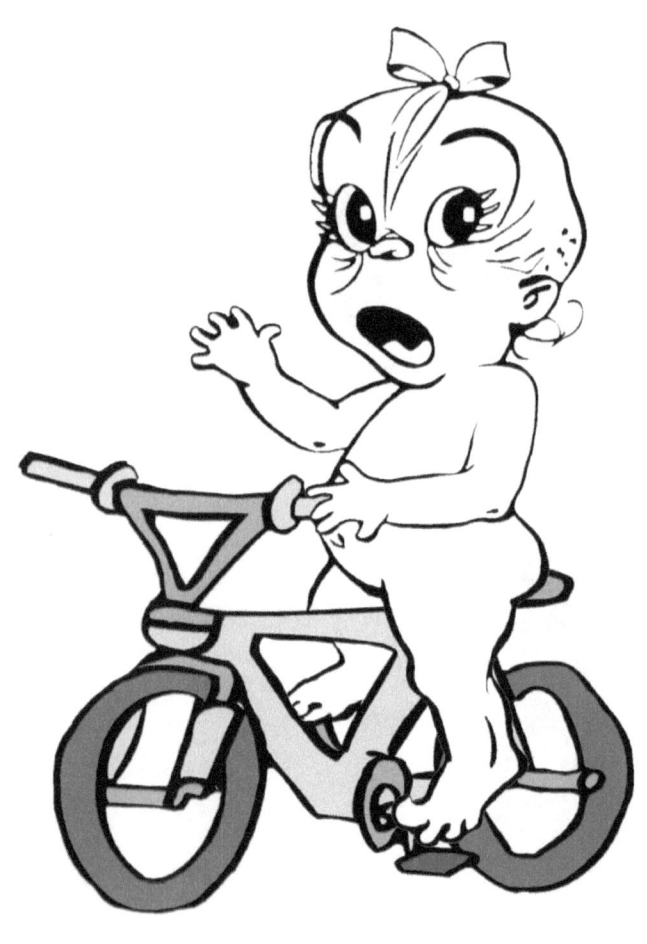

GETTING READY FOR THE
TOUR DE FRANCE

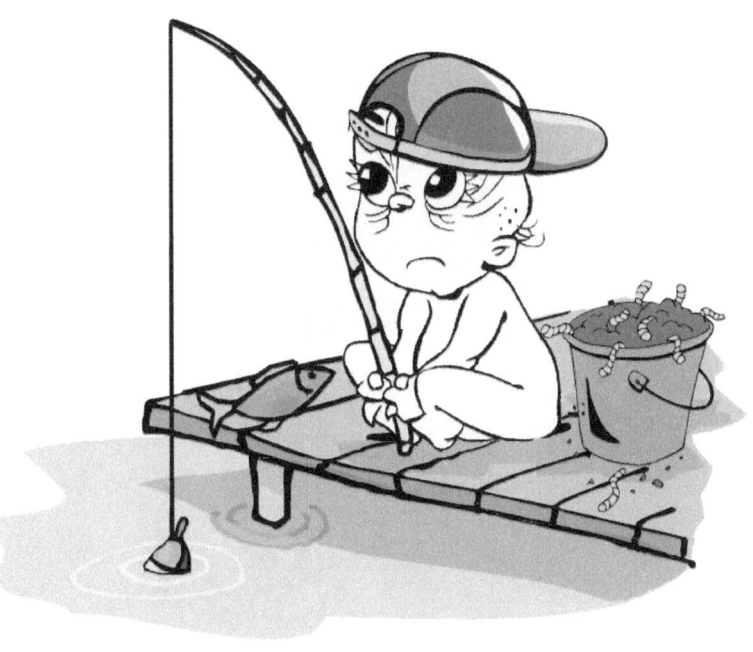

THEY SAID THIS WAS FUN ...
I DON'T EVEN <u>LIKE</u> FISH !

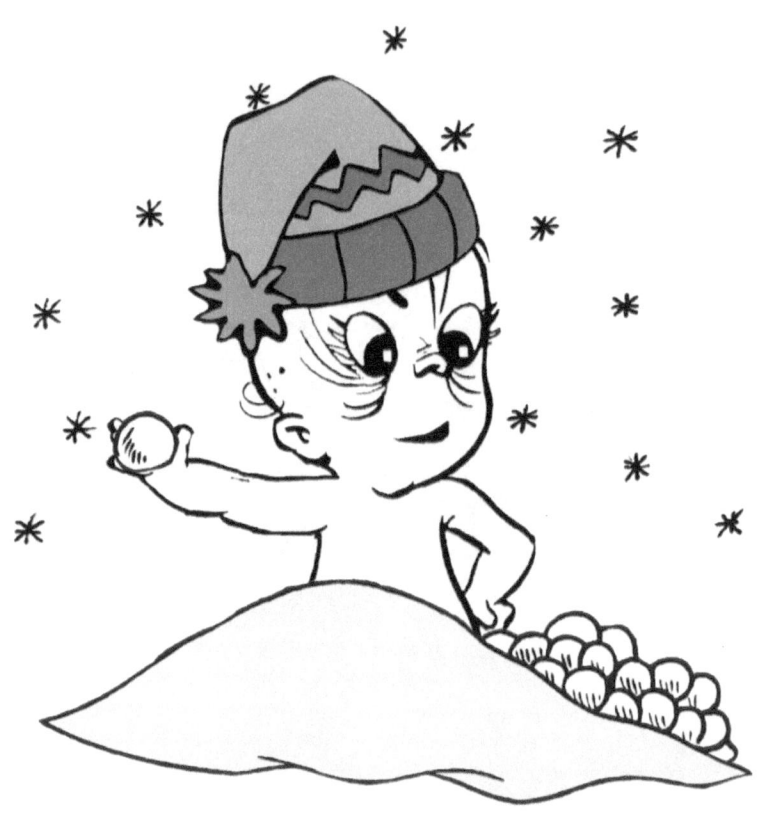

HEH, HEH! SIS DOESN'T KNOW ABOUT
MY STOCKPILE OF SNOWBALLS!
I CAN HAVE AN AMBUSH !

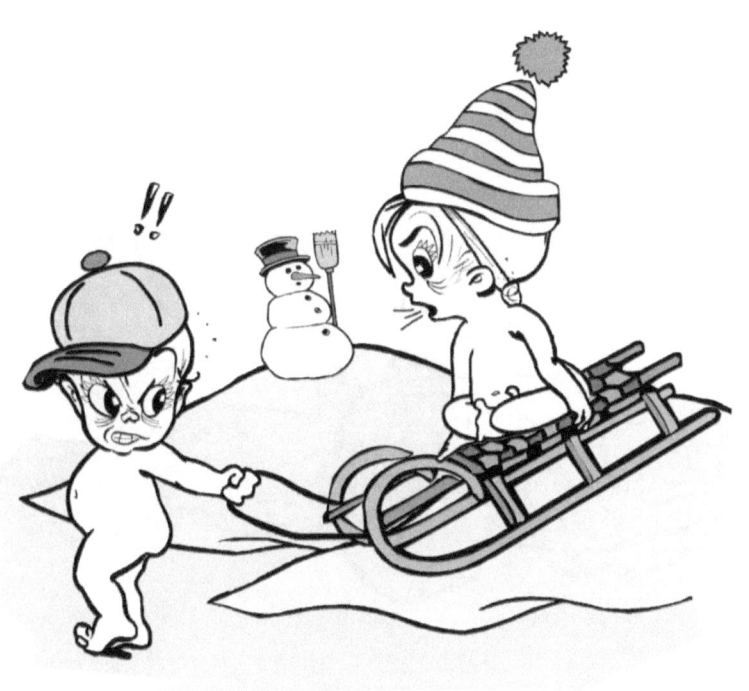

AW, YOU'RE JUST MAD BECAUSE I
BEAT YOU DOWN THE BIG HILL AND
NOW YOU HAVE TO PULL ME HOME!!

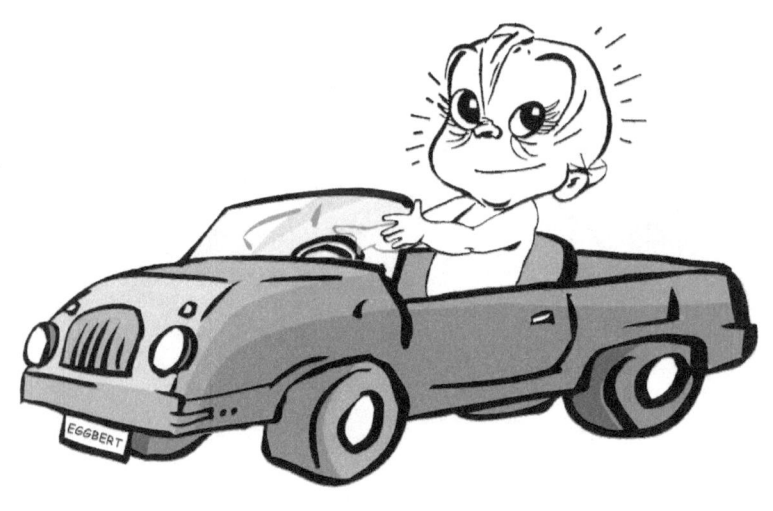

POP SAYS SPORTY CARS LIKE THIS
ARE GREAT CHICK MAGNETS !

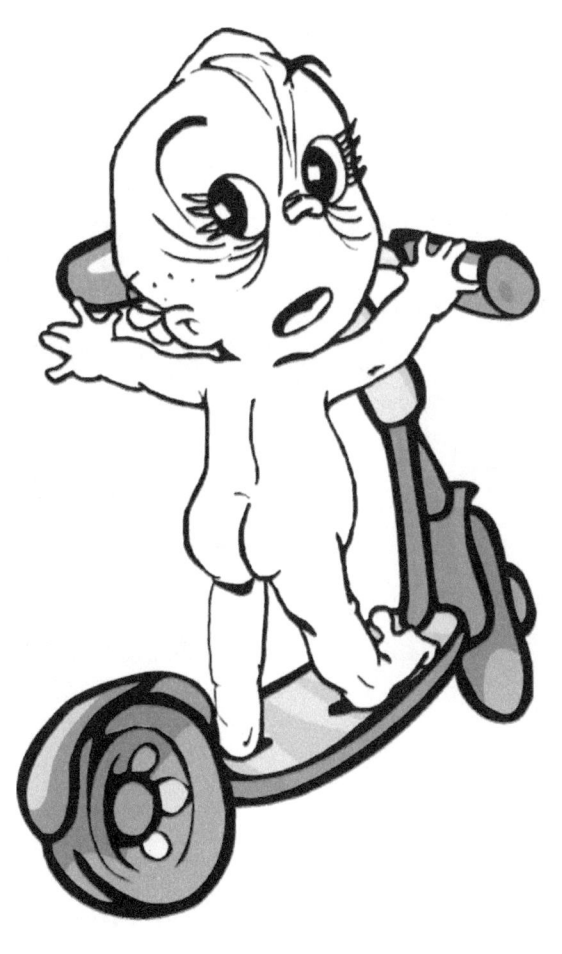

HEY, POPS! WHERE'S THE MOTOR??
THIS AIN'T A HARLEY !

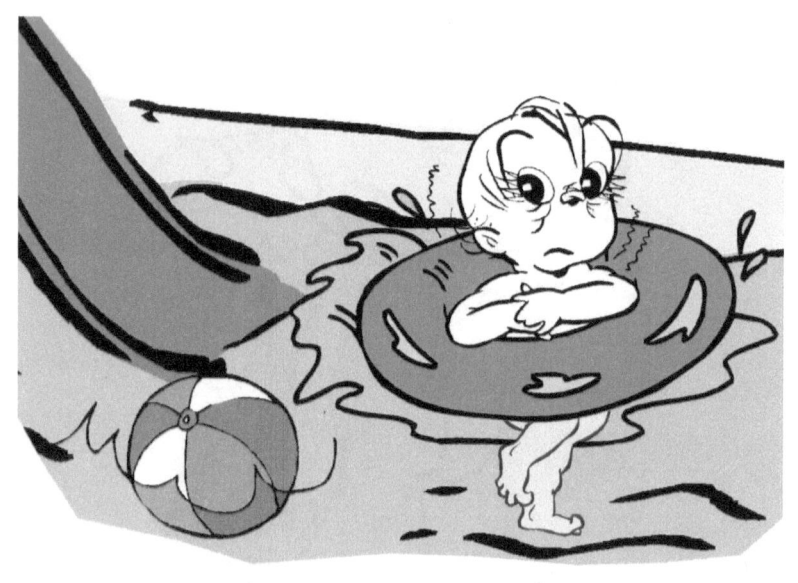

HEY, MA ...
CAN I GET OUT NOW?
I'M ALL WRINKLEY!

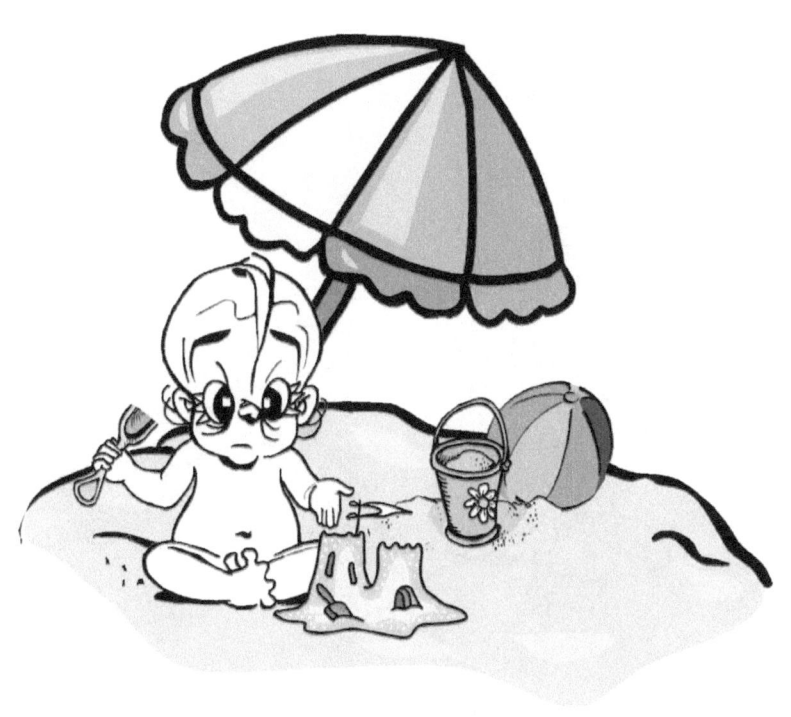

I NEED A BUILDING PERMIT
FOR <u>THIS</u>?

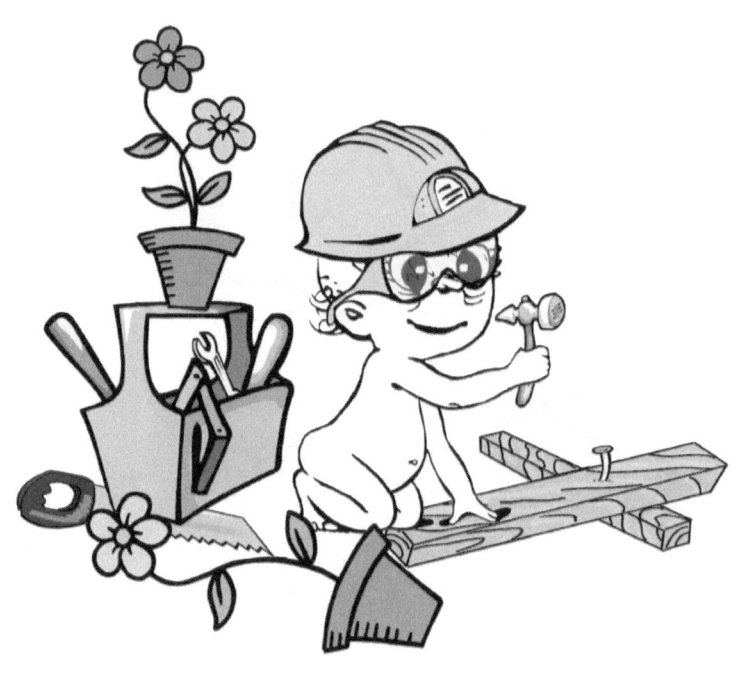

I SURE HOPE MA LIKES HER
NEW FLOWER BOX!

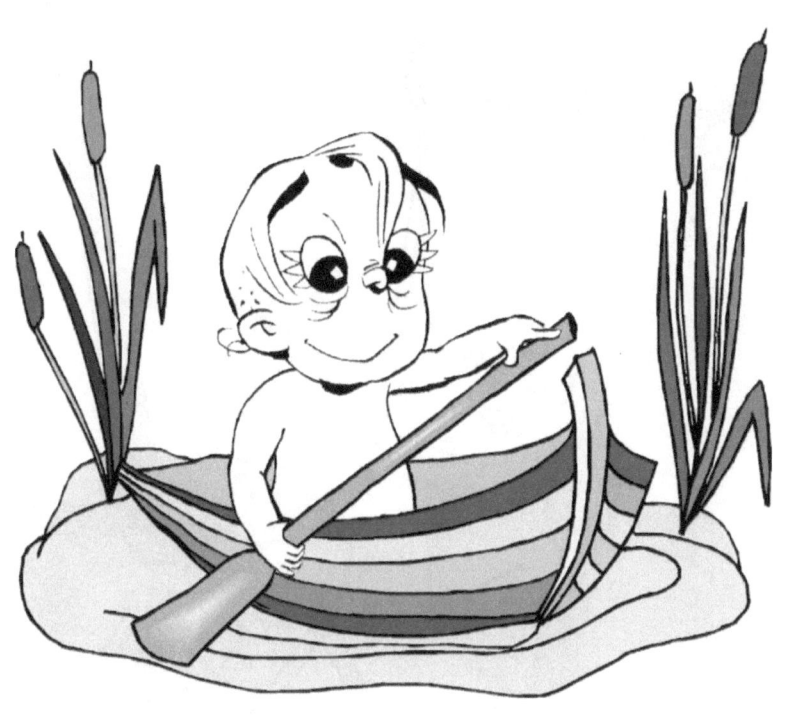

IT'S NO YACHT, BUT IT WORKS FOR ME.
(AND IT'S SO SMALL, EGGBERTA
WON'T GET IN IT ! HEH, HEH!)

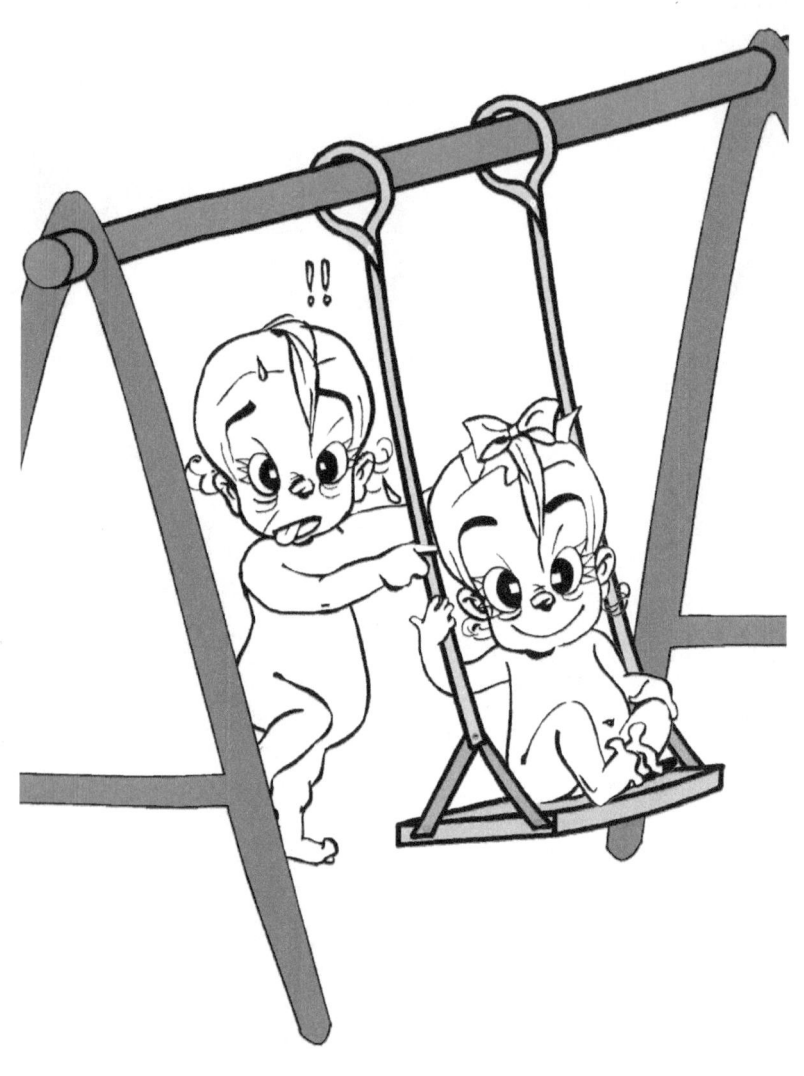

GEE, SIS ...
YOU NEED TO LOSE A LITTLE WEIGHT!

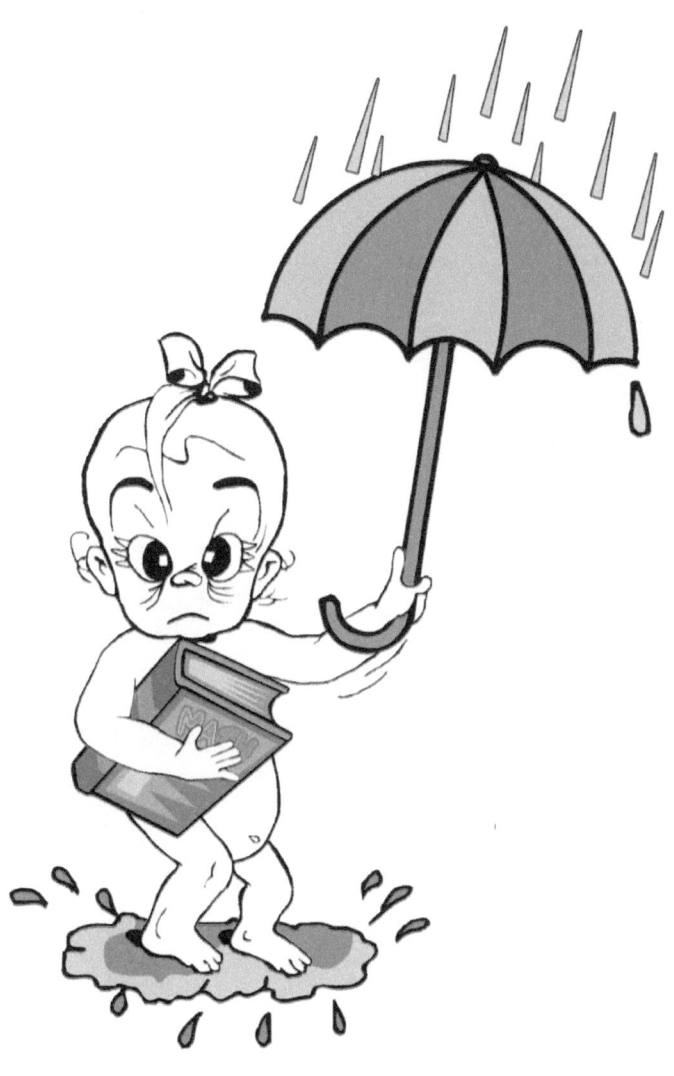

JUST THINK ... GENE KELLY
DANCED IN RAIN PUDDLES AND
MADE IT LOOK LIKE <u>FUN</u>!

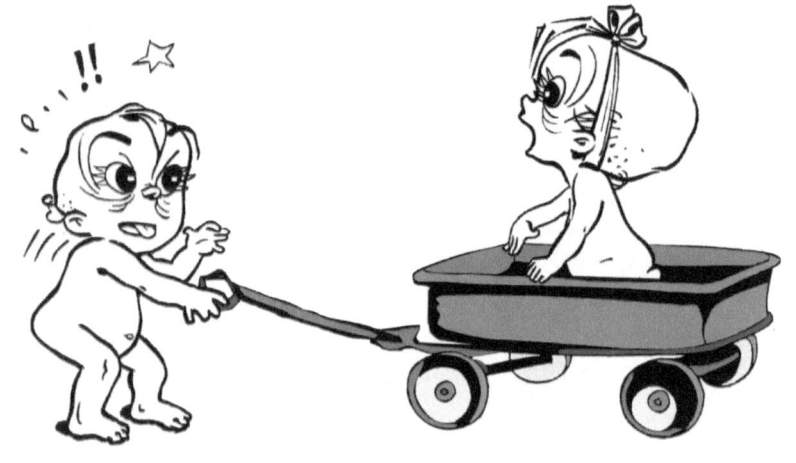

FASTER, FASTER!
I WANNA GO <u>FASTER</u>!

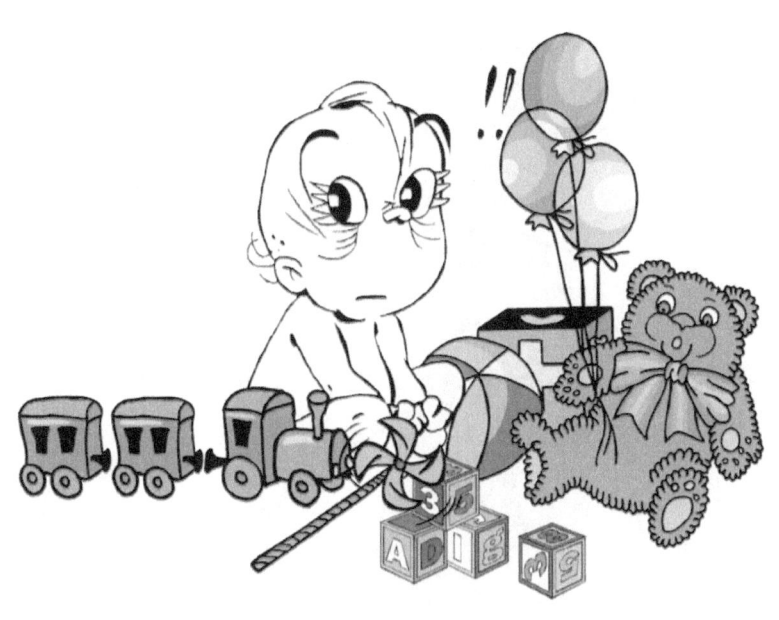

SO MANY TOYS ... SO LITTLE TIME !

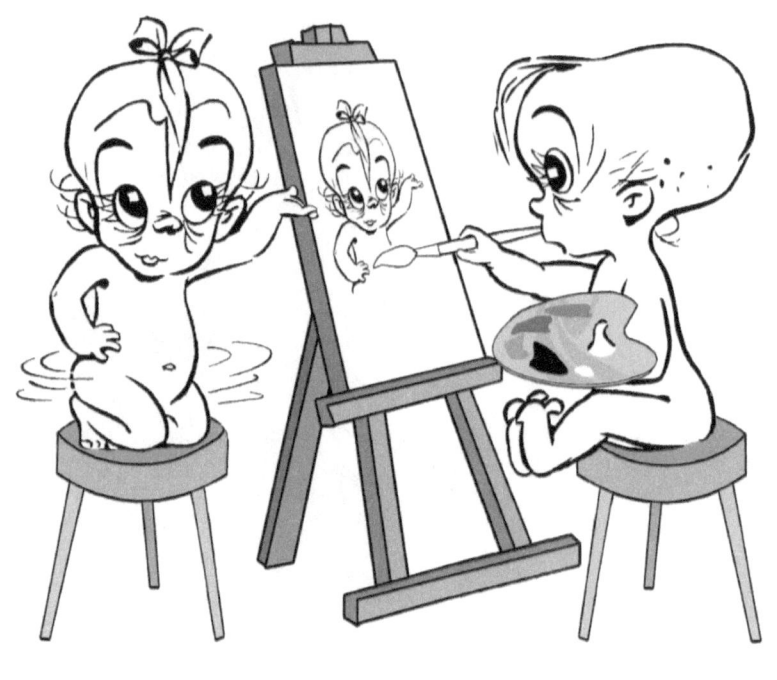

AW, C'MON SIS ...
SIT STILL!